Maximising the Impact of Teaching Assistants in Primary Schools

Drawing on the lessons from one of the world's leading research and development efforts on and involving teaching assistants (TAs), this book is the authors' most authoritative text yet on how to design a whole school plan to improve TAs' deployment, practice and preparedness, and put it into action. The authors use robust theories and original research to explore an innovative and integrated approach to making the most of TAs, and recognising the valuable contributions they make to the classroom and the school.

Structured around a unique and empirically sound conceptual framework, this book provides essential principles, practical tools and workable strategies, developed through collaboration with hundreds of UK schools. It focuses on ensuring TAs can thrive in their role, and presents the tools and techniques needed to do so accessibly, and is illustrated with case studies on school and classroom practices.

Essential reading for all primary school leaders and SENCOs responsible for training and managing TAs, this book is also a useful resource for teachers and teaching assistants looking to optimise the TAs' contributions.

Used in combination with *The Teaching Assistant's Guide to Effective Interaction*, *Maximising the Impact of Teaching Assistants in Primary Schools* is a comprehensive and unrivalled guide to supporting school workforce improvement.

Rob Webster is an Associate Professor at UCL Institute of Education, London. He researches and writes about special educational needs and inclusion, and he developed the Maximising the Impact of Teaching Assistants programme.

Paula Bosanquet is a Senior Teaching Fellow in special educational needs at UCL Institute of Education, London. A former primary teacher, she has worked extensively as a trainer with teaching assistants, schools and local authorities.

Sally Franklin was a Senior Teaching Fellow at UCL Institute of Education, London, and now works as a SEND consultant, supporting schools in the UK and internationally.

Matthew Parker was a Senior Teaching Fellow at UCL Institute of Education, London, and now works as a school improvement consultant and expert advisor for inclusion.

'Any leader looking to maximise the impact of teaching assistants in their school should read this book immediately. Reassuringly, there are no 'silver bullets' or quick fixes, but instead countless practical strategies underpinned by years of detailed research. Rather than simply providing a list of 'what works', the authors go deeper and show how schools have made these changes work. Crucially, they clearly understand schools, and are realistic about how lasting change can be brought about. I have no doubt that this book will quickly be seen as the definitive guide to deploying teaching assistants effectively.'

James Bowen, Director of Policy, National Association of Head Teachers (NAHT) and Director of NAHT Edge

'Never before has it been more important for senior leaders to strategically and effectively deploy teaching assistants. This excellent book provides an essential and accessible summary of key evidence and research with practical recommendations for busy school leaders. The journey to maximising the impact of TAs lies within!'

Maria Constantinou, Co-Headteacher, St Mary's CE Primary School, Barnet, London

'Rob Webster and the MITA team have had a profound impact on TA deployment and practice across the country. This book will be no less transformative. Drawing on the latest research, with accessible and practical examples throughout, it should be mandatory reading for all primary school leaders.'

David Bartram OBE, Director, Prescient Education Ltd

'Primary schools invest a huge amount of time and money into teaching assistants, and rightly so. But do schools and school leaders make the most of this investment? This book is the most authoritative review I know of how to harness the talents and potential of this crucial part of our school workforce. Rooted in research and lessons learned from the large scale and respected MITA programme, it draws together key principles for success, offering really helpful examples of these principles being applied in a range of contexts. The authors are at pains to point out it not a manual; rather, it is a set of ideas that school leaders can implement in a way that works in their context. There is a deep acknowledgement running through the book that strong change processes are crucial here: the what and the *how* both matter. I cannot recommend this rich resource highly enough.'

Andy Buck, CEO, Leadership Matters

'Based on leading research, *Maximising the Impact of Teaching Assistants in Primary Schools* is a practical and extremely relatable insight into how schools have successfully developed and embedded the valuable contribution of TAs. This book is the ultimate read for any primary school leader looking to develop a whole school approach to effective TA deployment. Superb!'

Natalie Packer, SEND Consultant and former adviser, SENCO and primary headteacher

'As Daniel Willingham says: 'Our brains privilege story.' This valuable addition to the *Maximising the Impact of Teaching Assistants* library sees Rob and the MITA team expertly narrate authentic school experiences of leaders, bringing evidence alongside the strategic deployment of TAs in their schools. The insights generated and shared in this great book reflect and tell the real stories of in-school implementation. The journeys continue!'

Andy Samways, Director of Unity Research School

Maximising the Impact of Teaching Assistants in Primary Schools

A Practical Guide for School Leaders

Rob Webster, Paula Bosanquet,
Sally Franklin and Matthew Parker

LONDON AND NEW YORK

First published 2021
by Routledge
2 Park Square, Milton Park, Abingdon, Oxon OX14 4RN

and by Routledge
52 Vanderbilt Avenue, New York, NY 10017

Routledge is an imprint of the Taylor & Francis Group, an informa business

British Library Cataloguing-in-Publication Data
A catalogue record for this book is available from the British Library

Library of Congress Cataloging-in-Publication Data
Names: Webster, Rob, 1976- author. | Bosanquet, Paula, 1971- author. |
Franklin, Sally, 1978- author. | Parker, Matthew, 1983- author.
Title: Maximising the impact of teaching assistants in primary schools :
a practical guide for school leaders / Rob Webster, Paula Bosanquet, Sally Franklin
and Matthew Parker.
Identifiers: LCCN 2020051442 (print) | LCCN 2020051443 (ebook) |
ISBN 9780367468330 (hardback) | ISBN 9780367468347 (paperback) |
ISBN 9781003031420 (ebook)
Subjects: LCSH: Teachers' assistants–Great Britain. | Teachers' assistants–Training of–
Great Britain. | Education, Primary–Great Britain.
Classification: LCC LB2844.1.A8 W43 2021 (print) | LCC LB2844.1.A8 (ebook) |
DDC 371.14/1240941–dc23
LC record available at https://lccn.loc.gov/2020051442
LC ebook record available at https://lccn.loc.gov/2020051443

ISBN: 978-0-367-46833-0 (hbk)
ISBN: 978-0-367-46834-7 (pbk)
ISBN: 978-1-003-03142-0 (ebk)

Typeset in Bembo
by Taylor & Francis Books

Contents

Illustrations

Acknowledgements

As with the previous titles bearing the 'Maximising the Impact of Teaching Assistants' name, we have, throughout this book, reflected the real-world views and experiences of schools with which we have had the privilege of working. The principles, process and strategies contained in this book have been developed, field tested, refined and improved through the hard work of school leaders, teachers and TAs, too numerous to list, and to whom we are greatly indebted.

The main purpose of this book is to tell the story of implementing the Maximising the Impact of Teaching Assistants (MITA) programme through the perspective of a small number of primary schools. We are immensely grateful to the leaders of these schools, and their staff, who were kind and keen enough to let us share their journeys with a wider audience. They are:

- Alver Valley Schools, Gosport, Hampshire: Jill Roseblade (Executive Headteacher) and Kate Russell (Assistant Headteacher and SENCO)
- Crestwood Park Primary School, Dudley, West Midlands: Maggie Stowe (former Headteacher) and Amy Cooper (current Headteacher and former Deputy Headteacher)
- Cuddington Croft Primary School, Cheam, Surrey: Scott Maclean (Executive Headteacher) and Alice Kiddell (Head of School)
- Laureate Community Academy, Newmarket, Suffolk: Dave Perkins (Headteacher) and Kelly Ashford (Inclusion Manager)
- Shirley Manor Primary Academy, Bradford, West Yorkshire: Heather Lacey (Headteacher) and Gail Whitmore (SENCO)

We are fortunate that a great many colleagues have recognised the value of MITA and, over recent years, have championed it in their own work with schools, local authorities, multi academy trusts, and on social media. We are hugely grateful to these colleagues – including those who have been kind enough to endorse this book – for their support and for helping to raise schools' awareness of our work.

We also recognise the hard work and contributions of several members of our MITA family: Kelly Golding, Aimee Shaw and Marina Kipfer. And finally, we extend our thanks to Jonathan Sharples, Senior Researcher at the Education Endowment Foundation, with whom we have worked for many years, and whose guidance and thinking on implementation has been invaluable in advancing and improving MITA.

Introduction

A thought experiment

Picture your school on a Friday. What are your team of teaching assistants doing? The likelihood is that most of them are supporting pupils in lessons; many of them working with pupils with special educational needs and disabilities (SEND). Some are outside the classroom, in a different learning area, a shared space or perhaps the corridor, delivering a 'catch-up' intervention, or giving some additional input to a small group of lower-attaining pupils to help their phonics or reading. There may be a TA delivering a therapy session for a child with speech and language difficulties, or working with a vulnerable child on managing their emotions. One TA might be telephoning a parent; another might be marking times-tables tests the class teacher administered the previous day. And another TA might be zipping around the school, gathering up some last-minute resources for an art activity, dealing with a first aid issue, or perhaps reuniting coats that have been left in the playground with their owners.

Now, imagine that all this is happening for the very last time. On Monday morning, your TAs will not be returning to school. How long would it be before their absence raised new or additional challenges for you, your teachers or your pupils? The majority of schools would most likely manage for the first week, but how many would make it to the end of a second week without severe disruption? What do you think the impact of having no TAs in your school would be after one month?

In autumn 2016, schools in Durham closed or were reduced to partial opening when over 1,800 TAs went on strike in protest against local authority proposals to fire TAs and reemploy them on lower-value, term-time-only contracts (Halliday 2016). Schools in Derby were similarly affected when TAs took the action to oppose council-made decisions that had reduced their salaries by up to 25 per cent (Harris 2016). In the early stages of the worldwide Covid-19 health emergency in 2020, the availability of TAs was the difference that enabled some schools to remain open to vulnerable pupils and the children of keyworkers during the spring/summer lockdown period (Speck 2020).

It is difficult to imagine any sector or industry maintaining service delivery quality when its workforce has been so heavily depleted. Thankfully, for reasons we shall come to, a future without TAs seems to us to be very unlikely. Yet the impact of a school losing its TA workforce even for just a day or two can be profound.

This example and the thought experiment above bring home the many important ways that TAs are embedded in the life, work and rhythms of a school. As we describe later, we have arrived at this situation over a relatively short period. But for many people working in schools, it is difficult to recall or imagine a time when TAs were *not* there. For school leaders especially, pausing to consider what would happen to your school if TAs suddenly 'disappeared' makes for uncomfortable thinking. Who will provide the individualised support to our most vulnerable children? How will our lower attainers keep pace with their peers and ensure they do not fall behind in developing basic skills? What about the dedicated time and nurture that our children with chaotic home lives so desperately need? And what about all the other vital stuff – mostly small, but indispensable – that keeps our teachers' workloads just about manageable?

We do not need to play out this imagined scenario any further to make the point that it would not take very long at all before teaching and learning and the wellbeing of pupils and teachers started to be negatively affected by the lack of TAs. TAs are the mortar in the brickwork; they hold schools together in numerous and sometimes unnoticed ways.

Introducing Maximising the Impact of Teaching Assistants

Despite its somewhat philosophical start, this book is not about theorising the effective use of TAs. It is a practical and relatable guide to helping primary school leaders rethink, repurpose, retool and reenergise their TA workforce. The principles and processes codified in this book are the result of one of the world's leading research efforts and reciprocal learning programmes on this topic, drawing on collaborations with hundreds of UK schools. It is the culmination of over 15 years of work and, we believe, the most authoritative text on TA deployment.

Specifically, this book is both the basis for and a product of the Maximising the Impact of Teaching Assistants (MITA) initiative, which reflects our learning from its application in schools. MITA – which we describe in detail in the next chapter – started out as a way of bringing to life and mobilising action around an earlier incarnation of this book, also called *Maximising the Impact of Teaching Assistants* (Russell, Webster and Blatchford 2013), and which in turn was the main output of an action research project with schools (Webster, Blatchford and Russell 2013). The experiences of schools involved in the first few years of MITA informed a second edition of that book (Webster, Russell and Blatchford 2016), which captured their experiences of implementing the processes and strategies covered in the first edition.

Since then, MITA courses and materials have developed and expanded, and been accessed by thousands of schools in the UK and overseas. The most significant development since the second edition has been that our approach to supporting schools to make the very best use of TAs has been formally trialled and tested for impact. So, for the very first time, we have robust empirical evidence of whether the 'MITA process' makes a difference to pupil outcomes.

This matters, because concurrent with the development of MITA has been the emergence over the last decade of what has become known as the 'what works' agenda. 'What works' describes the effort to promote the intelligent use of data and evidence to improve the effectiveness and efficiency of national education policy and learning outcomes for pupils. School leaders and teachers are increasingly consulting and evaluating research findings in order to inform strategic decision-making about what goes on in everyday classrooms. At the heart of what we are talking about is the effective targeting of effort; schools simply do not have the resources or capacity to invest in practices that do not add value or that lack evidence of impact.

TAs comprise just over a third of all people working in primary and nursery schools in England (DfE 2020). This requires serious and sustained investment at the national level, the middle tier level, and the individual school level. The system needs its leaders and decision-makers who are held to account to feel empowered to make decisions with confidence, so it is right that they should demand evidence of the effectiveness of the various things on which they spend public money.

This book draws on the latest research and our extensive experience of working with schools to apply the evidence via the MITA initiative, in order to help primary school leaders address, with confidence, the question of 'what works' in relation to the effective management and deployment of TAs. It builds on key principles, processes and strategies contained in our earlier work, which we have refined and improved through further collaborations. Our work with schools has also added to our store of practical examples, and you will find the best of them in this book.

The early part of this book will take you through the evolution of MITA, the evidence base that underpins it, and the research *on* MITA; that is, what we have learned from independent evaluations of our programme of school workforce improvement and training. Tempting though it might be to flick to the chapters that describe the MITA process (i.e. what to do), we recommend you take the time to read this opening chapter, because the principles, processes and practices that make up the bulk of this book flow directly from the research on TAs. This coverage will help you obtain a secure grasp of the 'evidence' part of our evidence-based approach. Also, an understanding of and engagement with the evidence will support you with the first stage of the MITA process: ensuring your staff buy in to what you want to achieve. As we shall see, a careful exposition of the evidence on TAs is a key part of our approach; not just in terms of convincing you to act, but crucially in bringing your staff with you. We will come to all this in due course, but let us continue this short introductory chapter by outlining the purpose of this book, its key features, and some pointers on how it can be used.

The purpose of this book

The main purpose of this book is to set out for primary school leaders a comprehensive process for reviewing and making changes to the ways your TAs are prepared and deployed. This book draws on learning and lessons from hundreds of primary schools that have applied previous iterations of our guidance and materials. As such, we have used this collective experience to improve and refine our overall approach and its various elements, and set these out here in a series of relatable and actionable recommendations.

We illustrate all of this with real world examples from regular primary schools (just like yours) that have fully implemented MITA, and which have emerged as some of the most effective and impressive schools we have worked with. The work these schools have achieved exemplifies an important overarching point about MITA, which is that there is no 'one size fits all' solution. However, while each of these schools arrived at creative, local solutions to the general and specific issues identified through the research evidence on TAs that were relevant to their context, the strategies they developed and the processes by which these came about are highly likely to apply, to a greater or lesser extent, in your school.

Although we have drawn all this into one place, this book is *not* a manual. The illustrative examples it contains are precisely that: examples. You need to think of each example as the output of a process that worked for that school, for their context, for their staff, and for the community it serves. Seldom will a practice, explained in isolation from its context, import neatly into another setting. This book will prompt you to think about *what* specific principles and processes of the MITA approach might look like in your setting, and *how* you might generate and embed them. Because it is so critical, we pay specific attention to matters of implementation.

Key features of this book

Schools are busy places. Time and funding are tight, and the pressure is always, always on. In this context, the urgency to improve outcomes, perhaps for a specific cohort or profile of pupils, means that doing 'what works' has obvious intuitive appeal. But in the rush to put new ideas in place, school leaders can be at risk of losing sight of how changes will be introduced, managed and sustained. Overlook this and in no time at all, a project initiated with the best of intentions can fade away as staff struggle to manage competing priorities. 'Initiativitis' causes fatigue, so to avoid depleting the funds of goodwill that new projects require, it is essential to practise good implementation.

Our experience tells us that as essential as knowledge of 'what works' is, it is only part of the process of adopting, shaping and embedding evidence-based practices. In order to unlock the full potential of the 'what', school leaders need good information on the 'how'. That is why in this book, we not only share great practices, we lift the lid on *how* schools have put them into place. Knowledge of implementation can help you assess if and how well particular ideas might transfer to your setting. We hope that in reading this book you are already partly won over by the promise and potential of MITA. However, what really matters is how it manifests itself in the day-to-day work of your staff. The difference between the schools that implement MITA more effectively and less effectively is *how* they strategise and operationalise its principles and practices. A key feature of this book, then, is that we guide you not only through what works, but *how* it works.

The foundation of the principles on which MITA is based is the result of extensive and innovative research, plus a lot of academic thinking and practical discussion. This work produced a conceptually and empirically strong framework for structuring decisions and action, the importance and value of which is understood and shared by school leaders, policymakers and researchers alike. We have been fortunate to share our work with all of these people, nationally and internationally, and these conversations continually shape what we do and how we do it.

By far the greatest influencers of and contributors to MITA's continued development are people like you. In our experience, putting the evidence on TA effectiveness into the hands of school leaders has a strong catalysing effect. It is the vivid and relatable examples harvested from schools, and which appear throughout this book, that makes MITA come alive and inspire others. A second key feature of this book, therefore, is that it gives primacy to describing the practical applications and exemplifications of MITA, which have emerged through its extensive implementation and validation in the real world.

School leaders that fully engage with the MITA process realise early on that the work of TAs has a far greater and deeper reach into the life of the school than they initially perceived. The 'mortar in the brickwork' analogy is so evocative precisely because when you imagine life without TAs (as we asked you to do on the first page) it brings to mind all the things that become harder, if not impossible, to achieve without them. A third feature of this book, therefore, is to consider the role of TAs in relation to key areas of policy and practice, such as the SEND Code of Practice and staff workload and wellbeing.

We believe that there is intrinsic value in the TA role, and we know that many schools share this view. We tend to find, therefore, that the argument that their full potential is not being realised is often enough to sell the MITA process to the governing body and the school staff. However, we know from experience that getting *every member* of your school workforce on board can mean leaders have to make the same case for action, but in different ways. Some members of your teaching staff, for example, might not be sufficiently motivated or feel empowered to prepare and deploy TAs effectively; they might be of the view that this is the responsibility of the SENCO. But if you can demonstrate how supporting a process of reform can ease their workload and improve pupil outcomes, you are more likely to win them over. We will outline the potential benefits of undertaking MITA, which you can use to frame the case for change to your staff and governors.

Using this book

This book is aimed at the people in primary schools who make the strategic decisions about TAs, namely headteachers and senior leaders. It is also highly relevant to SENCOs and inclusion managers who, depending on the school they work in, may also have a senior leadership position. Leaders in all-through or secondary schools may additionally wish to refer to an earlier iteration of this book (Webster, Russell and Blatchford 2016), which includes additional guidance specific to settings serving pupils in Key Stages 3 and 4.

If you are a school leader and you have picked up this book with a view to rethinking and reforming the way you use TAs in your school, we would first like to commend you for taking this matter seriously. No doubt you will already be aware this is no small task, but, as we have been emphasising in this opening section, it is a vital one if schools are to make the most of their TAs and have a positive impact on learning. Before we go any further, it is worth making some key points that we have learned about leadership in relation to MITA.

Leading change

Once exposed to the research evidence on TAs, we find that headteachers are willing to consider the implications for their schools. However, not all recognise that because of the wide-reaching strategic decision-making implications, it is imperative that they drive the process. It is understandable that given competing pressures, action gets delegated to a middle leader or to the SENCO who is not necessarily connected to, or reports directly to, the senior leadership team (SLT). This can mean that change is piecemeal and sometimes puts the staff who have been delegated the responsibility for change in a difficult position, particularly if this requires taking decisions they do not have the power to take; for example, amending TAs' hours of work.

Neither can we assume that it is TAs alone that need to change. As we indicated above, so deep-rooted are the factors that determine TA effectiveness, it is unrealistic – not to mention unreasonable – to expect TAs to solve the problem of their use in schools through their efforts alone. So, while we entirely agree that TAs, like teachers, should have access to regular training to increase their knowledge and improve their practice, this alone is not sufficient to remediate the effects of longstanding, foundational aspects of their employment and deployment.

We noted earlier that hundreds of schools have undertaken MITA and accessed our guidance and resources. The various campaigns, projects and initiatives with which we have been involved have given us opportunities to work closely with schools. Indeed, this book is the product of a small number of deep, sustained and fruitful collaborations with local clusters of schools in several regions of England. A consistent feature across the schools with which we have worked with most closely is that the involvement of the headteacher is critical to success. Put simply, to avoid neutering the effects of the impact you can potentially achieve from the process outlined in this book, it is essential that change is sanctioned and led from the top by the person who has the greatest decision-making powers: the headteacher.

Make time and take time

If there is one other thing that unites the schools we have worked with, it is they recognise that change takes time. Schools that undertake the MITA programme plan, pilot, develop and evaluate progress over two or three terms; for the most committed schools, however, it is a project lasting at least two years. Some schools can spend at least a term unpacking and getting a handle on the extent of the issues in their school. There is no right or wrong way here; the speed and distance of travel depends on your starting point, and this naturally varies from school to school.

Headteachers often tell us that they wish they could move at a quicker pace, but speeding up the process invites trouble. Do not get despondent if you think progress is slow or things take longer than you expected. Getting to grips with current practice is always time well spent, because it is the foundation for getting the future direction right for your school and securing and maintaining buy-in from staff.

Be sure to set aside regular time throughout the school year to focus on the project. Think of MITA as a process, not a one-off event. Again, a key piece of learning based on the feedback from schools is that MITA works best when integrated into the strategic plans for school improvement – built in, not something bolted on to existing priorities. This matters when it comes to maintaining the backing and buy-in of your staff; commitment soon slides if teachers and TAs think of MITA as 'another thing they have to do', rather than as an intrinsic element of their professional practice.

Finally, we find that when schools reflect on the MITA process, they remark that it is time that is the key commodity. So – and it is worth making this point early in the book – it is the investment of time, attention and effort into improving practice that seems to make the difference, not spending lots of additional money.

Be sensitive

These are turbulent times. Media reports about spending cuts and redundancies, amplified and refracted through chatter on social media, and overlaid onto individuals' personal circumstances can lead to MITA taking on an entirely different meaning. Our change and improvement process may be called Maximising the Impact of Teaching Assistants but it is not unheard of for some TAs in some schools to think that MITA is an elaborate ruse to remove them from their posts altogether.

This is unhelpful, but understandable. TAs feel the precariousness of their role, in terms of its contingency on, for example, SEND funding (CooperGibson Research 2019). School leaders must be tuned in to the context into which MITA is introduced, and act with sensitivity. TAs who fear that MITA could threaten their job security will be lost to the process before it begins.

Later in this book, we discuss how you can pitch the benefits of MITA to your staff and convince them of its value, importance and potentially transformative impact. However, it is worth saying here that, as leaders, you need to ensure your messaging regarding MITA is straightforward and clear, and delivered with care. You must be alive to the possibility that no matter how clear *you* think your message is, there may well be several members of your TA team who are concerned about what it means for their lives and livelihood.

Finally, let us be really clear: we did *not* write this book to justify or support a process of staff rationalisation. If there is a prospect of your school needing to reduce TA numbers or their hours of work, we recommend addressing this *before* you commence MITA.

SEND provision

Chapter 4 of this book covers undertaking a review of current TA deployment and practice. In our experience, this process tends to raise questions about the ways in which schools meet the needs of pupils with SEND. TAs have become deeply connected to the way schools organise provision for SEND and, as the research we shall discuss in the next chapter has shown, there are inherent risks in assuming that TAs are either the *only* option or the most *appropriate* option for meeting the needs of some of our most vulnerable pupils.

The audit procedure and the process of change described in this book could be enhanced by, or conducted as part of, a wider review of school structures and processes connected to SEND provision. The key point to make here is that MITA can, indeed should, be a component of reviewing and making improvements to your SEND provision, but it is *not* a substitute for it.

Key recommendations for school leaders

- The whole process of review, consultation and change *must* be led by the headteacher.
- Give yourself at least two terms to conduct your preparatory work, with a view to rolling out a full school-wide strategy from the start of the next school year.
- Schedule regular meetings to discuss the planning, development, implementation and review of your approach.
- Take a consensual approach. Ensure everybody has the opportunity to have their voice represented.
- Be clear about your motivations for undertaking the MITA process – especially with your TAs. Make it clear that this is about improving the structures and processes within which they work, in order to maximise their contribution to the school.
- Consider undertaking MITA as part of a wider programme to review and improve your SEND provision.

Other audiences for this book

We hear time and again from staff in schools that teachers are given very little guidance on working with TAs through either their initial teacher education (ITE) course or school induction (see below). Given that virtually every primary school teacher works with a TA, this is a state of affairs that lets down everyone: teachers, TAs and pupils.

One of the aims of this book is to support senior leaders and SENCOs to put in place induction and training arrangements for teachers in order to equip them with knowledge and skills to improve the way they work with TAs. That said, many of the techniques and strategies we describe can be put into place directly by individual classroom teachers. There is much teachers can do to improve their practice, which is not dependent on the leadership team undertaking the broader strategic process. In this sense, this book can be considered required reading for all teachers: from PGCE students and trainees undertaking school-based routes to qualified teacher status, to recently qualified teachers and experienced practitioners. This book will also be useful to teachers who are considering a move into leadership.

The levels of preparedness of newly qualified teachers (NQTs) to direct and work with TAs is revealed in data from the annual NQT survey. These surveys (Pye, Stobart and Lindley 2016; Ginnis et al. 2018) consistently report that, of all aspects of their preparation for teaching, deploying classroom support staff is one of the areas in which NQTs in England feel least prepared.[1] TAs also report that teachers lack an understanding of their role (CooperGibson Research 2019). There is, then, a clear challenge for ITE providers when it comes to ensuring new teachers are confident and competent in working with TAs. Therefore, teacher training providers and those involved in the delivery of professional development can use material in this book to inform and support a range of training and courses. We have written this book in such a way as to be accessible to practitioners and those that work with them. The material contained herein can be used to support professional development and in-service training.

While this is not a book about SEND, we know that previous iterations of this book have appealed to educational psychologists (EPs). As we have written elsewhere, EPs have a pivotal role in supporting schools and parents in the transition to alternative practices for pupils with SEND, which are less reliant on near-constant TA support (Webster 2014), and in providing training for TAs (Bosanquet and Radford 2019).

Finally, decision-makers at the regional and national level responsible for policy and practice regarding classroom support staff will also find this book relevant to their work. At the school level, governors and trustees will find much to inform their thinking. We also anticipate that this book will be of interest to educators and policymakers outside the UK, given that more and more countries are introducing TAs to support inclusion in mainstream schools.

The Teaching Assistant's Guide To Effective Interaction: How to maximise your impact

The audience we have not yet mentioned is, of course, teaching assistants. While this book has not been written for TAs, there is guidance available specifically designed to dovetail with the philosophy, principles and practices we cover in this book. Our response to the need for practical guidance for TAs is *The Teaching Assistant's Guide To Effective Interaction: How to maximise your impact*, by Paula Bosanquet, Julie Radford and Rob Webster.

C̶o̶n̶...work the...this book, *The Teaching Assistant's Guide...* clarifies the
rol̶...the TA as unique...t from, but complementary to, that of the teacher. It
f̶...on the pivotal...role of TAs' talk and interaction with pupils in the
...*Teaching Assistant's Guide...* opens out and develops
...of Chapter 6, which gives school leaders a flavour of the approaches in our
...e. Each book is aimed at a different audience, but the messages and practices are
...t and complementary.

...the emphasis on the practical, *The Teaching Assistant's Guide...* contains training
and development materials for TAs, which can be used as the basis for school-based inset,
to support formal courses for TAs (e.g. foundation degrees), and by individual TAs.

Underpinned by key theory and research, and written in a highly accessible manner, it
provides a clear framework to guide and support TAs to refine or develop the skills
required to scaffold learning effectively and to encourage pupils to become more independent. It contains lots of reflection activities, practical strategies and techniques for TAs
to use and try. In the same way as this book and its predecessors underpins our MITA
programme, so *The Teaching Assistant's Guide...* is the basis of school-based training for
TAs and teachers, called Maximising the Practice of Teaching Assistants (MPTA).

We cross-reference to *The Teaching Assistant's Guide...* and MPTA at relevant points
throughout to give you a sense of how they interrelate with this book and the MITA programme. Indeed, taken together, the two books and the complementary training demonstrate how the path to transforming the way your school uses TAs, and to ensuring they make
a distinct and valuable contribution to learning, requires taking action at different levels.

Contents of this book

We very much hope you enjoy reading this book, but our principal reason for writing it
is to provoke action. We want you to *use* it. This book aims firstly to stimulate your
thinking, and secondly to support you in taking practical steps to improve the effectiveness of TAs and the ways in which they are deployed in classrooms. We sometimes refer
to this process as the 'MITA journey'. We hope that once you have read this book, you
will feel inspired and equipped to begin yours.

We conclude our introductory chapter with a short precis of the other chapters in this book.

Chapter 1: The case for change: Why primary school leaders need to rethink the role and contribution of TAs

As we noted earlier in this chapter, before we progress much further, it is important to
lay out the evidence that underpins our evidence-based approach. In this chapter, we
chart the short history of the TA role and describe findings from key research studies of
their deployment and impact that have informed the development of MITA. A main aim
of this chapter is to make a compelling case for why school leaders should review and
rethink the role and contribution of TAs. We introduce an instinctive conceptual framework to structure both the theoretical and practical, and the strategic and operational
aspects of this work.

We then describe the MITA programme and its core principles. We provide a short
history of its evolution, and our work with schools, so that you can see how we arrived
at the processes and practices covered in the main body of the book. We finish by

considering the political and educational context, and raise some important points for you to hold in mind as you proceed.

Chapter 2: Setting your vision

This chapter encourages and supports you to take the first steps toward developing a clear strategic vision for the deployment and practices of TAs in your school. We introduce a framework for leading and embedding change that underpins the process of successful implementation, which we look at in detail in Chapter 3.

We will consider how the current vacuum in terms of government policy and accountability processes provides ample opportunity for action, and explain how MITA connects with the bigger picture of addressing educational inequalities.

We describe the first steps of the 'MITA journey' and give you some ideas for beginning to establish for yourself the role, purpose and contribution of TAs in your school.

Chapter 3: Implementation journeys: The most important chapter of this book

It may seem flippant to subtitle this 'the most important chapter of this book', but the reason we have done this is to convey the significance of thinking through the implementation of MITA – and to leave you with no excuses for skipping this section!

We wanted to make matters of implementation much more explicit and more detailed than in any of our previous writing on this topic. Our work with dozens of schools has convinced us that the effectiveness with which school leaders manage the change process is one of the best indicators of whether the changes that they introduce are accepted and supported by staff, and whether new impactful practices are successfully embedded and sustained.

Before we reach the chapters that describe 'what works', we consider *how* to get it to work. We will describe how to bring coherence to the work outlined in subsequent chapters by drawing on the experiences of a small number of schools we have got to know well. We use the framework from Chapter 2 to describe how these schools operationalised MITA and brought transformational change to their settings. Illustrative quotations from the school leaders will bring the process to life and provide early inspiration for the programme of work laid out thereafter.

Chapter 4: Reviewing current practice

This book encourages you to undertake work that will, in all probability, involve some degree of organisational change. Knowing the position from which you start is central to any project that takes you to a specified end point – your vision. This short chapter, therefore, sets out a process for reviewing the way you currently use TAs, which you can use as your baseline.

We provide the tools and guidance to help you evaluate key aspects of TAs' employment, deployment and preparation – all of which have been developed for the MITA programme and been field-tested by thousands of staff in hundreds of schools.

Chapter 5: Supplementing, not replacing, the teacher: Deploying TAs differently

Decisions about TA deployment are the starting point from which all other decisions about TAs flow. It is from here that we begin the work of acting on your vision by considering alternative models for deploying TAs. Detailed guidance and exemplar strategies and approaches are founded on two key principles: firstly, that TAs should not be used as an informal teaching resource for lower-attaining pupils and those with SEND; and secondly, that TAs should be deployed in ways that add value to what teachers do, not replace them.

Chapter 6: TAs' interactions with pupils: Scaffolding for independence

Chapter 6 centres on the fine point of a particular model of deployment, which we believe harnesses the true potential of the TA role: as scaffolders of learning. It provides an entry-level view of the work that is fully expressed in *The Teaching Assistant's Guide to Effective Interaction*, discussing the concept of scaffolding and introducing the framework at the heart of our sister publication, which supports TAs in their interactions with pupils. This chapter provides specific supplementary guidance on how to implement, embed and sustain new practices to support scaffolding for independence.

Chapter 7: The preparedness of TAs: Improving their readiness for the role

Whatever roles you decide you want TAs to perform, you need to ensure that they are adequately prepared to carry them out. Chapter 7, then, considers the decision-making relating to preparedness: providing opportunities for professional development and for planning and feedback between teachers and TAs. Using examples from real-world settings and common situations, we explore and provide workable solutions to some of the persistent problems of preparedness.

Chapter 8: Maximising the impact of structured interventions delivered by teaching assistants

The MITA programme centres predominantly on the role of TAs inside classrooms, but this book would not be complete without a discussion of, and guidance on, the deployment of TAs to deliver structured interventions and catch-up programmes. In this chapter, we cover how to review the programmes and processes of curriculum interventions, and how to optimise the role and impact of TAs in their delivery.

Conclusions

Our final chapter draws together some key messages and general conclusions about implementing the MITA process. We share some indications of impact, based on our extensive work on supporting schools to improve the deployment, practice and preparedness of their TAs, and consider the broader implications of our work in relation to the evidence-based drive to educational improvement.

Note

1   The other areas that NQTs consistently rate having low confidence on are teaching pupils with SEND and teaching pupils with English as an additional language.

Chapter 1

The case for change

Why primary school leaders need to rethink the role and contribution of TAs

Background

The increase of, and increasing interest in, teaching assistants

In the Introduction, we referred to the role of 'what works' in educational improvement; that is, the use of research evidence to inform decision-making and practice. The foremost 'what works' organisation in England is the Educational Endowment Foundation (EEF). The EEF amasses, synthesises and curates research evidence for the practitioner audience via its Teaching and Learning Toolkit. The What Works Clearinghouse performs a similar function in the USA, providing a repository of 'high quality research' on 'different programs, products, practices and policies', which supplies practitioners with the information they need to make 'evidence-based decisions' (What Works Clearinghouse 2020).

Since its launch in 2011, the EEF Toolkit has become central to – and indeed instigated (Coldwell et al. 2017) – evidence-based practice in schools. According to the EEF's own data, half of all school leaders in England consult the Toolkit to inform decision-making (EEF 2018).

A consistent feature of debates about 'what works' in schools has been the role of teaching assistants and their impact on pupil attainment. The Toolkit categorises TAs as a 'high cost, low impact' resource, based on evidence showing not only a limited impact of TA support overall, but a disproportionately *negative* effect for the most disadvantaged pupils – specifically, lower attainers and pupils with SEND (EEF 2020). We shall dig deeper into this evidence momentarily.

While teachers and school leaders subscribe to the notion that findings from research can improve practice, this assessment of the empirical evidence on TA impact – which is echoed in the influential work of John Hattie (2015) – has attracted much attention, and provoked strong reactions and some resistance. The main reason for this reception is that the evidence is at variance with many practitioners' experiences and expectations. Teachers place considerable value on having an additional adult in the classroom to provide individualised attention to struggling pupils while they attend to the rest of the class (Blatchford, Russell and Webster 2012). Any evidence that calls this value into question, and may in turn make TAs' position precarious – a possibility to which England's overworked teachers are highly sensitive – is likely to perturb.

As we argued earlier, it is hard to dispute that the entire edifice of inclusion has become reliant on TAs. They perform a valuable and tangible function on which schools depend, and which survives in the face of counterintuitive and perhaps inconvenient evidence of a detrimental effect on the learning of the most disadvantaged pupils. Evidence carries little weight too when factoring in the human and political cost of removing or considerably reducing a large chunk of the school workforce; a constituency comprised predominantly of women in part-time, low paid work.

From parent-helpers to an integral part of the school workforce

The part-time nature of the TA role is a legacy of how it originated in the UK. We can identify three particular influences over the last 30 or so years. The earliest influence was the increased involvement of parents in school life, which led to a surge in volunteer helpers. In the early 1980s, some schools (mainly infants and primaries) had as many as 50 parents a week providing assistance (Caudrey 1985). As well as providing a much-needed extra pair of hands for activities such as school trips and art, parent-helpers also helped with a particularly time-consuming task for teachers: the teaching of reading. The essential need for children to develop this basic skill in order to access the curriculum, coupled with the fact that hearing readers (arguably) requires little in the way of training, perhaps explains why support from additional adults was directed towards this task.

Alongside these developments there was a second key factor driving the increase in school support staff. Following the 1981 Education Act, which enshrined rights for pupils with SEND in law and put duties on local authorities and schools to make provision for these pupils, there was an increase in the number of pupils with SEND being taught in mainstream settings.

The drive towards inclusion had a profound effect of changing not only the composition of the pupil population in mainstream schools, but also the composition of the school workforce. Volunteer arrangements were formalised into salaried positions as 'welfare assistants' and 'special needs assistants', and latterly 'learning support assistants' – all of whom worked almost exclusively supporting pupils with SEND. Other parent-helper roles evolved into general 'classroom assistant' and/or 'teaching assistant' posts. There was, however, no consistency in how these 'assistant' job titles were applied across schools. Over time, people in these roles came to be known collectively as 'teaching assistants': a catchall title to refer to all classroom-based and pupil-based support staff.

Thomas (1992) concludes that the increase in the number of, and frequency with which, additional adults came to work alongside teachers in the classroom between the 1980s and 1990s happened largely 'by stealth'. The number of 'non-teaching support staff' grew as schools welcomed the offer of assistance from parents. It was perhaps inevitable that with so many willing volunteers, some were deployed to undertake (or drifted towards doing) instructional tasks. Again, this support was targeted at the pupils with the greatest need.

The third main driver of the increase in support staff came in the early 2000s. In response to concerns over excessive teacher workload and the knock-on effect this was having on recruitment and retention, the government put in place a set of provisions to help schools manage teacher workload by freeing up time for planning and assessment, and removing routine, time-consuming administrative tasks. The National Agreement (DfES 2003) enabled and encouraged schools to employ more TAs and other support staff, such as bursars, reprographics staff, site managers and examinations officers, in order to help deliver these provisions for teachers. A key expectation of and justification for this policy was that the use of support staff would lead to improvement in pupils' academic outcomes.

The increase in school support staff can be seen as part of a general rise in para-professionals across the public services, not just in the UK, but worldwide. Professional roles in education and other sectors (e.g. medicine, social work, law, police) have been redefined, so others (e.g. nurses and paralegals) undertake some activities previously performed by established professionals (Bach, Kessler and Heron 2004). Encouraging evidence from England and Wales has shown that where TAs absorb some of teachers' administrative burden, it can have a positive impact on their workload and stress levels (Blatchford, Russell and Webster 2012).

The general effect of these initiatives over the last three decades has been that TAs now occupy a role in mainstream schools where they interact with pupils – principally those with SEND and those not making the expected levels of progress. On the face of it, this may look like a good arrangement, because TAs provide more opportunities for one-to-one and small group work, both in and out of the classroom. However, as we will see, it has also led to unintended consequences for pupils on the receiving end of that support.

While the widening use of 'non-teachers' is the result of pragmatic and well-meaning responses to particular needs at the school level, the evolution of the TA role has profoundly changed the dynamics of classroom interaction (Webster 2015). Furthermore, this has, to a large extent, occurred with little debate or public discussion, or recourse to the evidence of the impact of TA support on pupils' learning.

Education systems across the world have seen sizable and sustained increases in TA numbers (Giangreco et al. 2014; Masdeu Navarro 2015), but nowhere has the growth in TAs been more pronounced than in the UK. Over the last 20 years, the number of TAs in mainstream schools in England has more than trebled. TAs comprise 35 per cent of the primary and nursery school workforce (DfE 2020). On the basis of headcount data, there are more TAs in these settings than teachers: 271,464 vs. 249,149. Add in TAs working in secondary schools and specialist settings (13 per cent and 52 per cent of the respective workforces) and the total number of individuals employed as TAs in English schools reaches 382,886. For perspective, this is roughly the population of Croydon (London's second most populous borough), and comfortably greater than the population of Iceland.

As our earlier thought experiment was designed to show, we have evolved to a position where divesting of TAs is highly problematic. For school leaders, TAs have become a highly relatable and tangible exemplification of the challenge of doing 'what works'. But this challenge has been compounded by a persistent complication: for a long time, we have been uncertain and unclear about what *does* actually work.

The evidence on the impact of TA support

When it comes to the research on the direct impact of TAs on learning outcomes, we can separate much of it into two broad categories: (i) studies measuring the effects of curriculum interventions and 'catch-up' programmes (e.g. reading, phonics) delivered by TAs, which are very often delivered outside the classroom; and (ii) studies focusing on how TAs are deployed inside the classroom under everyday conditions.

TA-led interventions

Simply put, there is good evidence pupils make progress in literacy and numeracy as a result of structured interventions delivered by TAs – but *only* when TAs have been properly trained to deliver those programmes (see Alborz et al. 2009; Sharples, 2016; Slavin, 2016).

The international evidence (Nickow, Oreopoulos and Quan 2020) on one-on-one and small-group instruction delivered by TAs is remarkably consistent. One of the most important, though underappreciated, findings from UK research relating to TA-led interventions is how great the impact on learning often is. The EEF has been leading the way on this, having funded (at the time of writing) 12 evaluations of TA-led interventions. Ten of these have shown a positive impact[1], which, in the context of most EEF trials yielding an inconclusive result (Sharples 2016), is a phenomenal success rate.[2] Pupils in these trials made, on average, between two and three months' additional progress compared to those in a 'business as usual' condition. What is more, additional work by Gorard, See and Siddiqui (2017) shows particularly positive effects on learning for children in disadvantaged groups.

As a school leader who cares deeply about improving outcomes for pupils, you will no doubt see the obvious appeal here. While results from well-designed randomised controlled trials (RCTs) do not imply certainty of success when applied to your own setting, they can improve our level of confidence when it comes to making good decisions about using a particular intervention and replicating the conditions under which it has been shown to work best. We will look in more detail at how to maximise the impact of TA-led interventions in Chapter 8.

TAs in everyday classrooms

Compared with TA-led interventions, the evidence on the impact of how the majority of TAs spend the majority of their time – supporting *inside* the classroom (Blatchford et al. 2012; Farrell et al. 2010) – tells a different story.

There are only a few studies that have systematically measured the direct impact of TA support on pupil attainment under normal classroom conditions; that is, separate from any specific impact from TA-led interventions. The large-scale UK Deployment and Impact of Support Staff (DISS) project, conducted between 2003 and 2009, found a *negative* relationship between the amount of TA support pupils received and their academic progress (Blatchford et al. 2012). This effect was found consistently in year groups across the four Key Stages and across the core subjects of English, mathematics and science. And the effect was most marked for pupils with the highest levels of SEND (Webster et al. 2010).

Other UK studies have found that pupils with SEND assigned TAs for support made less progress than their unsupported peers, in both literacy and maths (Klassen 2001; Reynolds and Muijs 2003). Evidence from another large-scale study that considered the effect of having a TA in the classroom – the Student Teacher Achievement Ratio project, conducted in Tennessee, USA in the 1980s – found no beneficial effect on attainment on pupils in kindergarten through to Grade 3 classes (ages 5 to 9) (Finn et al. 2000). Longitudinal research from the UK Class Size and Pupil-Adult Ratios project produced similar results (Blatchford et al. 2004).

There are very few RCTs that investigate the impact of TAs in everyday classrooms, but two conducted in Denmark have found mixed effects (Masdeu Navarro 2015). However, there were insufficient data on school leaders' decision-making and classroom practices, meaning it is difficult to conclude what drove the effects.

Secondary analyses of school expenditure have suggested the expenditure on TAs is positively correlated with improved academic outcomes (Brown and Harris 2010; Nicoletti and Rabe 2014; Hemelt and Ladd 2016). However, these analyses of TA impact do not adequately rule out the possibility that other school factors (such as demographics) might explain the correlations found, and the conclusions drawn are often not supported by the evidence collected; in particular they do not include data on *what actually happens* in classrooms.

An early attempt to measure the impact of applying evidence-based guidance on TA deployment (to which the MITA team contributed) in nearly 1,000 primary schools across Yorkshire found encouraging signs that it had a mild positive impact on pupil attainment in English at Key Stage 2, but not in mathematics (Sibieta and Sianesi 2019). However, the finding should be treated with caution, due to the small size of impact measured (an improvement of 0.03 standard deviations compared with a synthetic control group) and the possibility that changes to the assessment and curriculum at Key Stage 2 during the evaluation period could have biased the results.

A central theme in the corpus of admittedly limited research into the impact of TA support on learning in everyday mainstream classrooms is that there is not yet any robust and consistent evidence showing a *positive* impact on pupils' academic outcomes. Accordingly, practical guidance for school leaders, including that set out in this book, starts not from the basis of provably 'what works', but from what has been shown *not* to work. With this as our starting point, we now draw on the wider findings of the DISS project to explain why the impact of TAs in the classroom is limited.

Explaining the impact of TA support in everyday classrooms

We might reasonably assume pupils who were given the most TA support in the first place would have been those most likely to make less progress in any case. However, in the case of the DISS project, such explanations, in terms of pre-existing characteristics of pupils, were unlikely. This is because the factors that typically affect progress and the allocation of TA support, such as SEND status, prior attainment and measures of deprivation, were controlled for in the statistical analyses. Therefore, to be of any consequence, any potential factor causing or influencing this relationship would need to be systemic across *all* year groups and *all* subjects, and related to *both* pupil attainment *and* the allocation of TA support.

Another possible explanation for the negative relationship is that it may be due to the different levels of TAs' qualifications relative to teachers. We note, however, that research has not found that teachers' or TAs' levels of qualification are related to their effectiveness (Muijs and Reynolds 2001; Blatchford et al. 2004; Wiliam 2010).

So, if pupil factors and TAs' qualifications do not appear to be explaining the negative relationship between TA support and pupil progress, what is? We argue, on the basis of data from the multi-method DISS project, that the most compelling explanation can be found in the decisions made by school leaders (and also, but to a somewhat lesser extent, by teachers) about how TAs are deployed and prepared for their role. The critical point, worth repeating, is that it is *not* the decisions made by TAs that is the issue here. In this sense, none of this is their 'fault'.

The DISS research team developed a conceptual framework made up of five components, called the wider pedagogical role (WPR) model, to explain the troubling impact results

(Webster et al. 2011). Firstly, the routine *deployment* of TAs in a pedagogical role can lead to a separation effect, whereby lower-attaining pupils and those with SEND receive less teacher input compared with their peers. Subsequent research has found this separation effect to be especially acute for pupils with an Education, Health and Care Plan (EHCP). A large-scale observational study found that the educational experiences of these pupils in both primary and secondary settings is characterised by a high degree of separation (Blatchford and Webster 2018). Compared to their average-attaining (non-SEND) peers, pupils with a Statement (now an EHCP) attending primary school spent the equivalent of over a day a week away from their classroom. As a result of a high level of support from TAs – the so-called 'Velcro' effect – these pupils spent less time in whole-class teaching with teachers, and were more than three times more likely to interact with TAs than with teachers. They also had about half as many opportunities to interact with their peers compared with average-attaining pupils.

Secondly, data from the DISS project found that TAs' *practice* (specifically, their interactions with pupils) tended to focus on getting tasks completed – and completed correctly. The quality of instruction pupils received from TAs was, therefore, markedly lower compared to that provided by the teacher. The TAs' role was reactive, and they tended to close talk down and 'spoon-feed' answers (Rubie-Davies et al. 2010; Radford, Blatchford and Webster 2011). Over time, this weakens pupils' sense of control over their learning and reduces their capacity to develop independent learning skills. As pupils, in effect, 'outsource' their learning to a TA, they develop learned helplessness.

The WPR model component of preparedness describes the lack of training teachers receive to know how to make the most of having a TA in their classroom, and the limited opportunities for, and quality of, planning, preparation and feedback between teachers and TAs. There was clear evidence from the DISS project that TAs frequently came into their role unprepared, both in terms of background training and day-to-day preparation. There were no specific entry qualifications for TAs and many did not receive any induction training. Relatedly, the vast majority of teachers reported having had no training in relation to managing, organising or working with TAs. In many schools, communication between teachers and TAs was largely ad hoc, taking place during lesson changeovers, and before and after school. Many TAs in the DISS project described 'going into lessons blind' and having to 'tune in' to the teacher's delivery in order to pick up vital subject and pedagogical knowledge, tasks and instructions. Preparedness is a persistent problem in many schools (Webster and Blatchford 2017).

We believe that the learned helplessness we referred to above is a function of ineffective deployment and preparedness. TAs act in ways that they perceive are helpful to pupils and which reflect favourably on their efforts (i.e. the amount of work a pupil completes in a lesson). The intentions are well-meaning, but this draws further attention to how TAs try to fill the vacuum created by an absence of clear guidance on, and preparation for, their role.

Far more distal to impact are the two final components of the WPR model: (i) TAs' *conditions of employment,* specifically their hours of work, which was connected to the limited opportunities for planning and liaison, and the tendency for TAs to meet with teachers in their own time; and (ii) TAs' *characteristics,* such as their age and experience (i.e. years in the role).

The WPR model was developed to explain the troubling results on academic progress found in the DISS project, providing a wider context within which to assess the effectiveness of TAs (in terms of pupil outcomes) and to take account of the factors that govern their employment and deployment – but over which they have little or no control. The WPR model, presented in Figure 1.1, shows how the components relate to one another. You will notice it is around the key concepts of deployment, practice and preparedness that the later chapters of this book are structured. We will, in each chapter, briefly outline key, relevant findings from the DISS project and other research on the role and impact of TAs. We do this to provide a solid empirical base on which to justify action and set out alternative strategies and promising approaches.

Maximising the Impact of Teaching Assistants programme

The Effective Deployment of Teaching Assistants project

Maximising the Impact of Teaching Assistants (MITA) started out as a way of bringing to life and mobilising action around an earlier incarnation of this book, the coverage of which was largely based on the Effective Deployment of Teaching Assistants (EDTA) project. The idea for this one-year action research project emerged out of conversations with educationalists and practitioners following the DISS project, and confirmed the belief there was a pressing need for clear, well-informed guidance on effective ways of deploying and preparing TAs.

The EDTA project involved researchers from the DISS project team working with 20 pairs of teacher-TA teams from ten schools (six primary, four secondary) in Hampshire and the London Borough of Islington. The three core components of the WPR model – deployment, practice and preparedness – were used as focal points of termly meetings. Participants were encouraged to develop small-scale trials to address one or more pertinent issues arising from the DISS project.

The team adopted a within-school comparative approach, evaluating practice before and after the introduction of the trials. They collected data using surveys, semi-structured interviews and quantitative structured lesson observations. The results of the EDTA project are available in Webster, Blatchford and Russell (2013), but a brief summary of the key points is provided below:

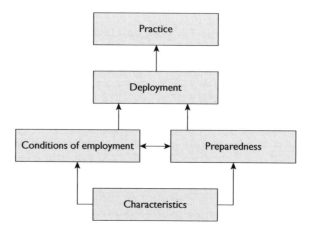

Figure 1.1 The wider pedagogical role (WPR) model

- Teachers were more aware of their responsibilities towards lower-attaining pupils and those with SEND, and worked more often with these pupils.
- There were improvements in the quality of TAs' interactions with pupils.
- Schools created teacher-TA liaison time.
- Teachers provided TAs with clearer and more detailed lesson plans.
- TAs' esteem, value and confidence improved from having a more clearly defined role.

Perhaps the key message for school leaders from the EDTA project was that changing the way TAs were deployed and prepared was not only possible, but had important benefits for *all* school staff and *all* pupils.

The MITA programme

Built initially around the WPR model, and arrived at via the EDTA project, the MITA programme is designed to help schools rethink how they deploy and prepare TAs, so as to mitigate and overcome the ineffective practices highlighted by the DISS project. MITA is a whole-school, whole-staff initiative, bringing together school improvement and professional development, which aims specifically to make improvements to TA deployment, preparation and practice. By dint of this, the extended aim of MITA is to improve pupil outcomes.

There are three integrated elements to the MITA programme, which are paced over two or three terms. MITA begins with a module for school leaders, which supports them through a process of strategic review and operational development to address head-on the common issues with classroom management, lesson planning and the way TAs interact with pupils. Starting from the evidence on the impact of TAs, we encourage, equip and empower school leaders to make fundamental and sustainable changes to practice at the whole school and classroom level. Coverage of the leadership module incorporates change management theory and implementation, as well as gap tasks, including the self-evaluation audit we outline in Chapter 4. The second component of MITA is individualised peer-to-peer support and challenge provided by an experienced school leader via regular consultancy visits to the school. This element of the programme is frequently built into our larger-scale projects and commissions within a specific region. Finally, there is our Maximising the Practice of Teaching Assistants (MPTA) training for TAs and teachers (see the Introduction). Typically, delivery is: two half-days of training for TAs, focused on how to scaffold learning and ensure their interactions with pupils foster independence; and a session for teachers (1.5 hours) centred on effective classroom use of TAs and a lighter-touch overview of the scaffolding training TAs receive. For more on MITA and MPTA, please visit our website: www.maximisingtas.co.uk.

In response to feedback from school leaders who participated in the early iterations of MITA, the coverage expanded to include guidance on implementation. An intermittent, though important, refrain in comments from some school leaders at the end of programme was that, while they felt well informed about the research and the practical implications, they wanted more support in terms of how to put the guidance into action.

At the same time as MITA launched, an increasing number of school leaders were learning of the DISS project findings through the EEF's Teaching and Learning Toolkit. The Toolkit's characterisation of TAs as a 'high cost, low impact' resource and the intuitive explanation of the DISS project findings resonated with school leaders' everyday experiences, and created something of a buzz in the sector. Inevitably, attention was focused on a question with which every school leader could identify: 'How do we best deploy TAs and avoid the ineffective practices highlighted by the research?'

As a consequence of this interest, we entered into a fruitful collaboration with the EEF to mobilise the evidence on TAs, which led to practical, actionable guidance report called *Making Best Use of Teaching Assistants* (Sharples, Webster and Blatchford 2018). A copy of the guidance was sent to every school in England. In swift order, it became the key resource on TA deployment. The positive reception it received prompted a reconfiguration of the MITA programme. The conceptual underpinning of the WPR model was retained, but the strategic advice and practical approaches were reframed and re-presented in terms of the headline recommendations with which school leaders were now somewhat more familiar. We will delve much deeper into these recommendations across subsequent chapters, but we have summarised them in Box 1.1.

Box 1.1 Recommendations for making best use of TAs (adapted from Sharples, Webster and Blatchford 2018)

The use of TAs in everyday classroom contexts

1   TAs should not be used as an informal teaching resource for low attaining pupils.
2   Use TAs to add value to what teachers do, not replace them.
3   Use TAs to help pupils develop independent learning skills and manage their own learning.
4   Ensure TAs are fully prepared for their role in the classroom.

The use of TAs in delivering structured interventions out of class

5   Use TAs to deliver high quality, one-to-one and small group support using structured interventions.
6   Adopt evidence-based interventions to support TAs in their small group and one-to-one instruction.

Linking learning from work led by teachers and TAs

7   Ensure explicit connections are made between learning from everyday classroom teaching and structured interventions.

Following the MITA process

This book details what we call the 'MITA process': the steps schools can follow to review and make changes to the ways they use TAs. We will guide you through the same process on which our strategic leadership course is based, introducing you to models, approaches, tools and ideas; and providing real-world examples of things that have been successful in schools we have worked with – and things that have not.

Briefly put, we will look at how to develop a clear vision on what you want the role, contribution and impact of TAs to be in your school (Chapter 2), and how to conduct a thorough audit of the current situation in your setting (Chapter 4). Over Chapters 5, 6 and 7, we discuss (respectively) approaches to deploying TAs, improving the quality of their interactions with pupils, and how to prepare them effectively for their roles in the classroom (as per the WPR model). These chapters map onto the first four recommendations of the *Making Best Use of Teaching Assistants* report. Chapter 8 considers the use of TAs to deliver structured intervention programmes, and corresponds to the three remaining recommendations.

A key aim for this book is to encourage you, as a school leader, to develop a clear vision for the TA workforce in *your setting*. We emphasise *your setting* because the MITA process is all about thinking through and implementing strategies and approaches that have the best chance of success in *your* school, for *your* staff and for *your* pupils. There is no 'one size fits all' solution; as a school, you will need to arrive at local solutions to the general and specific problems we have identified through our research and development work, and which may apply, to a greater or lesser extent, in your setting.

The overall standpoint of the book is to identify with the many school leaders who tell us that their schools would struggle to function without TAs, but also to show why progress can only be made if we first recognise there are problems with the current and widespread forms of TA deployment, and that alternative ways of utilising them need to be developed. We recommend you start with the end in mind. Effective leadership is all about defining a blueprint, gaining consensus around change and ensuring everyone within the school is working in ways consistent with bringing that vision to life. Our experience has shown that these are the 'active ingredients' in producing practices that stick. Schools that take the vision-defining step seriously tend to create favourable conditions for change; that is, staff get onside early, and stay onside. A key theme of this book is this: *changing the way you use TAs in your school is necessarily a leadership issue.*

We will come to this in due course, but an equally key message to emerge from our ten years of working to support schools in maximising the impact of teaching assistants is that, as the lead person for instigating, driving and overseeing the MITA process, you must focus at least as much attention on *how* it is implemented as on what is implemented. Implementation is the focus of the third and most important chapter of this book. For now, it is enough to say that while it tends to be the case that it is the 'what' in 'what works' that tends to attract school leaders' attention, it is crucial that you do not lose sight of the wider context and implementation process. This is what we mean by the 'how': the ways in which an intervention is operationalised and embedded, in order to ensure sustainable change and positive outcomes.

Good implementation wraps around and weaves through the MITA process. Implementation is particularly important for complex, whole-school interventions such as ours. As these processes function in addition to the WPR model, we deal with this early on in the book, so that you can use implementation as a lens for contemplating the guidance that follows.

We end this chapter on the case for change with some thoughts on the contemporary policy and practice context within which the implementation of MITA would occur.

The political and educational context

Getting issues relating to TA employment and deployment on the policy map has taken time. Despite mentions of our work registering in government guidance and briefings, and recognition for our public engagement and impact work (Webster et al. 2020), the reality is that national education policy remains largely oblivious to issues concerning

TAs. In our view, the failure of successive governments to develop a meaningful direction or state a position on what amounts to well over a quarter of the schools workforce seems somewhat remiss. Compared with teachers, there are no entry requirements (i.e. a minimum qualifications threshold), performance criteria, or national pay and conditions architecture for TAs or other support staff. Progress towards the latter was unfortunately curtailed in 2010.

While the policy gap regarding TAs concerns us, the good news is that school leaders do not need to wait for government edicts to take purposeful, positive action. Indeed, the direction of travel over recent years has been to devolve decision-making to individual schools. As we will see in the next chapter (setting your vision), the autonomy schools have is favourable to implementing MITA. We believe our work can be of great assistance to school leaders looking for a framework for change in the absence of a policy response.

There is a wider educational consideration here. We know lower-attaining pupils and those with SEND tend to be supported by TAs, rather than teachers. As Giangreco and colleagues (2005; 2010; 2021) have repeatedly argued, an implicit form of discrimination has developed: the most vulnerable and disadvantaged pupils receive less educational input from teachers than other pupils. If there are grounds for saying pupils with SEND are not appropriately served by this arrangement, there are also grounds for saying lower-attaining pupils are equally poorly served.

We are concerned that the failure to engage fully with the fundamental questions about the deployment of TAs, as evidenced by the DISS project findings and other research (see Chapter 5), reinforces longstanding models of practice that continue to let down disadvantaged children. Therefore, if we are serious about addressing the well-known tail of underachievement, we should take very seriously the experiences of lower-attaining pupils and those with SEND, and the way in which current models of deploying TAs may not be helping their educational progress as much as we may have thought. *That pupils are negatively affected by the very intervention designed to help them should on its own be a wake-up call to anyone with an interest in bringing about social and educational justice.*

An extreme take on the DISS project findings on pupil progress could be to drastically cut the number of TAs. Indeed, we have seen one-sided interpretations of our research cited in reports recommending just this in England (Woolf and Griffiths 2013) and the USA (Curliss 2014) as part of cost-cutting measures. However, as should be clear by now, this is not a position we endorse. In fact, we stand squarely behind the hundreds of headteachers who have told us, over and over, that without TAs, their school would not function successfully. Reframing the role and purpose of TAs is therefore essential to not only avoiding accusations of wasteful expenditure and a negative effect on pupil out-comes, but moreover, to making a strong case for giving TAs their own identity and value, demonstrable through measurable impact.

To restate one of our central messages: *the reasons why support from TAs has been found to have a negative effect on pupil progress is not the fault of individual TAs; it is the decisions made about TAs, not by TAs – starting at the school level with the headteacher – that are the issue.*

None of this should let policymakers off the hook, however. There are clearly wider system-level matters of importance at play, which are beyond the remit of any headteacher. For example, initial teacher education providers need to do more to prepare new teachers to be managers of TAs within their classrooms. This also extends to teachers' confidence and competence to work with pupils with SEND, and more broadly, understanding the difference between 'underachievement' and 'having SEND', and how this affects provision planning. There are also persistent problems within the broader SEND system that add pressure (see below).

We believe it is important to establish clear roles for teachers and TAs, and to develop the systems to support and maintain an appropriate demarcation, so that each role – though different and complementary – can be valued and respected on its own terms. As we have already indicated, it is also our strong belief that it is schools, not policymakers, that are best placed to undertake this work. When they do, as the book will demonstrate, change *is* possible.

To be successful, schools need clear, well-informed guidance – which is where this book comes in. The overall challenge facing school leaders is how to define the role, purpose and contribution of TAs, and show how it adds value to pupils' educational and social development in a distinctive way. The aim, as we see it, is to identify and implement ways in which the TA *adds value* to what the teacher provides, rather than replacing them.

A note on MITA and provision for pupils with SEND

It is worth saying from the outset that the work we outline in this book should *not* be seen as a proxy for rethinking how your school meets the needs of pupils with SEND. We say this because in some schools, TAs and support for those with SEND have become so enmeshed that a co-dependency has developed. This was evident in findings from both the DISS project and a subsequent large-scale study of pupils with high level needs in both primary and secondary settings (Webster and Blatchford 2015; 2019). When schools restrict the deployment of TAs to supporting pupils with SEND, they overlook: (i) other forms of support (e.g. more teacher input); and (ii) alternative roles for TAs.

The final crucial message of this chapter is that the aim of maximising the impact of TAs is *not* limited to the types of work TAs do to support pupils with SEND. Our aim is broader: we see TAs as having a potentially transformative effect by taking on the type of roles that can benefit *all* pupils. While the coverage of this book alights on the need for schools to improve SEND provision, we do not provide detail on, for example, the aspects of quality-first teaching such pupils need and deserve. Nonetheless, we strongly encourage you to develop a parallel line of thinking on other areas of your SEND provision, beyond matters relating to TAs, that might need to be reviewed and improved. Where appropriate, we will flag some useful references and resources that may help you with this.

Notes

1 Two of these trials were found to have no effect on learning
2 It is worth noting that this should not be characterised as any kind of 'failure', but indicative of a wider issue in relation to obtaining positive outcomes from randomised controlled trials conducted at scale in 'real world' conditions. Research projects undertaken by the EEF and its equivalent in the USA, the Institute of Education Sciences, show that despite the best possible conditions, around 80 per cent of projects do not return a positive impact on learning (Coalition for Evidence-Based Policy 2013).

Chapter 2

Setting your vision

Introduction

Unlocking the potential of your TA workforce begins with a fundamental provocation: what is the impact you want to see? Defining a clear strategic vision is a critical first step to maximising the impact of your teaching assistants. As you proceed with the MITA process, we will disrupt your thinking; we will challenge your perceptions about the *role, purpose* and *contribution* of TAs.

In this chapter, we consider some of the leadership fundamentals required to support the process of introducing school-wide change and how to make it stick. We describe the first steps of the MITA journey and, with reference to government policy, the 2015 SEND Code of Practice, and the Ofsted inspection framework in place at the time of writing (Autumn 2020), we consider the spaces that are available within which leaders can think anew about the role of TAs.

Making time to lead

As a primary school leader, you are in the important and privileged position of defining the strategic vision for your setting. You are responsible too for its actualisation; that is, putting in place the structures and procedures to enable your colleagues to play their full part in the drive towards realising that vision.

Your experience of school leadership may, at times, resemble a game of 'Whack-a-Mole': each time a task or issue is dealt with, another pops up somewhere else. You may feel that this firefighting draws your time and attention away from the less urgent, but no less important, strategic work that attracted you to leadership in the first place. Without noticing, leaders can become expert trouble-shooters adrift on a rudderless ship. It is important, therefore, to make yourself step away from the firefighting, and to commit time and effort to this first part of the MITA process: defining a clear vision.

In the early stages of this process, we recommend you schedule time with your leadership team to have open and unrestrained debates about current practice and to begin fleshing out your vision. School leaders that participate in the MITA programme value having the time away from school, as it gives them time and space to think and discuss without interruptions.

Steps to change

The MITA approach is underpinned by a framework developed by Harvard Business School academic, John Kotter (1995; 1996). Kotter's framework describes an eight-step process to bringing about and embedding lasting and transformative change within an organisation. Kotter's model is not without its critics (Appelbaum, Habashy, Malo and Shafiq 2012), and while it has a stronger theoretical base than an empirical base – a limitation it shares with almost every other change management model (Stouten, Rousseau and De Cremer 2018) – its usable format describes a sequence of steps that, in our experience, resonates intuitively with school leaders.

We have listed Kotter's eight steps below. We use these to mark out the stages of the MITA process throughout this book, and also as a way of structuring some important evidence relating to implementation, which we focus on in the following chapter:

Step 1. Establish a sense of urgency
Step 2. Create a guiding coalition
Step 3. Develop a clear vision
Step 4. Communicate the vision
Step 5. Empower people to act on the vision
Step 6. Create short-term wins
Step 7. Consolidate and build on gains
Step 8. Institutionalise the change

The first step is to establish a sense of urgency; that something must be done about a particular issue. The fact you are reading this book suggests you are already on the first rung of Kotter's ladder. Your sense of urgency may well have been ratcheted up a notch or two having read this far in; and it may increase further as you examine the realities of the situation in your school on the basis of the results of your audit (see Chapter 4).

This first step also involves identifying opportunities. As far as the MITA process is concerned, this includes taking a close look at things within the current educational milieu that can frame and inform your vision-setting.

Framing opportunities

At the end of Chapter 1, we made a point of saying that MITA is no substitute for addressing how your school meets the needs of pupils with SEND. It is important to decouple questions about the use of TAs from those about how schools meet the needs of pupils with SEND and those at risk of underachieving, which require responses that may include, but go beyond the use of TAs. This way of thinking is a core principle underpinning the MITA process and it avoids loading unrealistic expectations on what it can achieve.

There are two questions school leaders need to think about over and above efforts to rethink the role of TAs: (i) how does your school ensure quality-first teaching for pupils with SEND?; and (ii) how does your school organise and integrate structured interventions and catch-up programmes for pupils who are falling behind?

School leaders need to answer these questions independently of solutions that directly involve deploying TAs as an *informal* teaching resource on a routine basis. Let us be clear: we think TAs can have a role in working with lower-attaining pupils and those with SEND. But in order for these pupils to get the high-quality pedagogical input they require, the work of TAs must be *part of* a wider set of provisions, such as support from specialist teachers, more time with class teachers, assistive technology and peer supports.

The research evidence we reviewed in the previous chapter should be sufficient to compel us to realise TA support can no longer be the default, *or only*, option for struggling pupils. Indeed, this way of organising provision for pupils with the highest level of SEND on a one-to-one basis is now the subject of intense questioning (Giangreco 2021).

The two questions above are not addressed in detail in this book, but they do help us define the nature of related questions, such as how we ensure teachers organise classrooms effectively with TAs present, and how we might maximise TAs' contributions to lessons. We recognise that schools need to work within given parameters exerted by external influences. So let us take a look at the forces impacting on schools and, as Kotter (1995; 1996) says, identify the opportunities that might help us achieve our goals.

The 2015 SEND Code of Practice: 'Underpinned by high quality teaching'

A founding principle of the current SEND Code of Practice is that 'special educational provision is underpinned by high quality teaching and is compromised by anything less' (DfE/DoH 2015, p25). Although we cannot be certain, it is not unreasonable to assume that this notion of compromise owes something to the findings from the DISS project. Compared to previous iterations of the Code of Practice, the teacher's role and responsibilities are more tightly focused in relation to meeting the needs of children with SEND, and it is expressly clear on the lines of accountability:

> 'Teachers are responsible and accountable for the progress and development of the pupils in their class, including where pupils access support from teaching assistants or specialist staff'.
>
> (DfE/DoH 2015, p99)

Based on what we know from the research, we might replace the word 'including' in the paragraph above, with the word 'especially'.

As for TAs themselves, the Code of Practice makes no mention of their responsibilities in relation to pupils with SEND. This is an important point, because it means schools should not act in ways (intentionally or otherwise) that make or give the impression that TAs are directly accountable for pupil outcomes. So, the Code of Practice makes the teacher's role clear, but the TA's role remains somewhat vague.

Government policy

We mentioned in the previous chapter that national education policy has been persistently slow to respond to and incorporate TAs. Based on the inaction of the last decade, it would not be too farfetched to say that the government's policy on TAs appears to be not to have one.

TAs have, though, received some warm words in political contexts in the shape of a debate in the House of Commons in March 2014 entitled 'The value of teaching assistants' (Hansard 2014). The present education secretary, Gavin Williamson MP, whose wife works as a TA, has been said to be 'very sympathetic' to the role, and 'understand[s] the significant impact that teaching assistants can have on pupils' lives' (Speck 2019). However, the government's approach has consistently been 'hands-off'.

Perhaps the best example of this is from 2015, when the government decided against publishing a set of draft professional standards for TAs that *it* commissioned. The decision not to publish the standards was curious for at least two reasons. Firstly, they were always intended to be non-statutory, so neither the government nor schools were locking themselves into using them. And secondly, it turned out to be a peculiar own goal, because when the newspaper *Schools Week* published a leaked copy of the draft standards (Scott 2015), they proved to be not only remarkably uncontroversial, but received a warm and positive reception from unions, school leaders and TAs. In fact, it was by some way *Schools Week*'s most popular news story of 2015 (Schools Week 2015).

The government's response justifying the decision not to publish the draft standards (from the schools minister, Nick Gibb MP) reinforced the perception that the government was not all that interested in the role or status of TAs: 'The government believes that schools are best placed to decide how they use and deploy teaching assistants, and to set standards for the teaching assistants they employ' (Scott 2015).

So, there is opportunity here. As a school leader, you have the autonomy you need to address an issue that policymakers will not. You do not need to wait for permission to act.

Ofsted

One of the most common questions we get asked in relation to effective TA practice is: 'What do Ofsted inspectors want to see?' We have generally found this a difficult question to answer, not least because we have had nothing more to go on than the Ofsted inspection frameworks and guidance available to schools.

Consistent with the prevailing trend in the English education system of giving primacy to the transfer of knowledge from subject experts, we would expect the School Inspection Handbook (Ofsted 2019) to have more to say about the role of teachers than TAs – and indeed it does. Coverage of TAs in recent iterations of the inspection framework has been exceptionally scant, perhaps reflecting the government's non-interventionist approach. In fact, the framework in use at the time of writing (Autumn 2020) is one of the weakest we have seen on this issue. In fact, across the 97 pages of the Handbook, there are just two mentions of teaching assistants – and these are confined to footnotes.

Much like the SEND Code of Practice, the teacher's role is sharpened and clarified, but the TA's role is, by comparison, indistinct. We think school leaders should use the openness in the Ofsted guidance to their advantage. Because there are no specific expectations in relation to what inspectors are looking for, school leaders can occupy this space, giving the TA role legitimate, operational definition.

A good example of this is making the approach to TA deployment in your setting explicit to inspectors *before* they go into classrooms to observe. A number of school leaders have told us that inspectors have queried what TAs were doing during lessons, as there were extended periods when it appeared to them as if the TAs were not doing much at all. As we describe in Chapter 6, ensuring TAs create space for pupils to undertake tasks and avoid unnecessary interruptions are essential components of our approach to promoting independence. Priming inspectors for this will help them to understand such practices in context.

Summary

So where does this leave us? We know the widespread models of using TAs are ineffective, and that school leaders have the power and freedom to innovate. It is your responsibility to define the role and contribution of TAs in your school, and (should an inspector ask) provide the evidence that your decisions in relation to this have the intended outcomes – the measures of which you can also define. It is also your responsibility – not your SENCO's – to ensure teachers are responsible for the progress and development of pupils with SEND in their classes, as per the Code of Practice. Teachers themselves must take ownership of this too, as they are accountable for pupil outcomes.

This clarification and shoring up of roles and responsibilities concerning teaching and learning at the school level and classroom level opens up a space in which we can begin to imagine distinct and alternative, but complementary, roles for TAs.

A values-led approach

It is important to note that simply correcting for ineffective deployment of TAs and ineffective TA practice is not going to be enough to create the truly transformative change we think is possible. For example, encouraging teachers to plan a role for TAs in lessons is essential, but there must be some kind of effective feedback mechanism too. We explain how to achieve this in Chapter 7. Similarly, we cannot simply tell TAs not to spoon-feed answers to children; we must ensure their talk is replaced with something more purposeful. We address this in Chapter 6.

Put simply, we need to build a positive alternative to how we use TAs in schools, which must be underpinned by a clear vision agreed and set by the SLT, who then take decisions and drive action consistent with it. While we have staked out the territory in which to think and act in relation to policy, we do not mean to imply that school leaders should determine strategic decision-making only in relation to extrinsic forces. Compliance can lead to some rather perverse thinking and behaviour, such as doing 'what Ofsted inspectors want to see'.

Setting your whole-school vision for TAs should prompt you to think like a leader, not like a senior inspector. Moreover, this part of the process allows you to assert intrinsically positive values, such as equality and fairness, to ensure the implicit forms of educational inequality and the double standards that TA support has inadvertently come to represent (Giangreco 2003; Giangreco et al. 2005; Webster et al. 2010) are reversed.

Assembling a MITA development team

Introducing a new initiative in school means devoting attention, time and effort to specific, *additional* activities. The everyday busyness of school life can affect the capacity to run new projects, but having a dedicated development team can help by distributing the workload and responsibility (Sharples, Albers and Fraser 2019). Furthermore, a workforce fatigued by recent change, cynical of impact or already working at capacity will resist new initiatives. So, a development team can also act as a vehicle to build consensus and to bring about change.

Kotter's second step for bringing about change suggests forming a guiding coalition: a working party to lead the development of MITA in your school. This is a small group of staff willing to support your vision and to contribute to developing and testing strategies on the ground.

In our experience, the most effective MITA teams are led by the headteacher and at least one other member of SLT, plus the SENCO. In many primary schools, we find the second member of SLT and the SENCO is the same person. Membership of your team must extend to teachers and TAs. Schools we work with tend to include two teacher–TA teams from Key Stages 1 and 2, and if you have an early years provision, a pair from this phase too. Keep your group to a manageable size to ensure your initial trials are feasible to conduct and staff are not overburdened.

We suggest you have protected time for regular team meetings to discuss progress. Set dates for meetings months in advance – and stick to them! As we noted at the start of this chapter, the firefighting nature of running a school can mean it is tempting to 'bump' such meetings to attend to other matters. Try to resist this. There is a risk that if it happens too regularly or for reasons your staff do not think are fully justified, you could send an unintended message that improving TA deployment and the quality of TA support is not that big a priority.

You will require honesty and candidness from your team, but people in less senior positions may feel intimidated about speaking truth to power. Therefore, consider drawing up some protocols at your first meeting about how discussions will be conducted in order to protect participants and encourage an open and productive dialogue.

Developing a clear shared vision

Having set the context for the discussions, you need to develop a clear vision for your school. This is the third step on Kotter's model, and it will provide a basis for the steps of your action plan. It is useful to adopt the approach of starting with the end in mind; that is, defining the point you want to reach. Constantly referring back to this will inform and drive the developmental work on the ground.

We set schools in the MITA programme the task of thinking about where they want to be in the future. This is a task that you can do with your SLT and with your development team. Imagine you are two years into the future. Take an imaginary learning walk of your school. What do you see and hear that demonstrates you have improved your use of TAs? Think of these as success indicators of the changes you have made. Focus on different groups. What kinds of things are pupils saying and doing? Are they able to work independently for longer? What kinds of things are teachers and TAs doing more or less frequently? Are your TAs no longer spoon-feeding? What comments do you hear from parents – specifically those who have a child with SEND? Are they showing more independence at home? Keep discussions open and positive.

You may feel you do not need to do a visualisation exercise like this, and that is fine. However, what you really cannot avoid is discussing and formulating an answer to this crucial question:

- *What do you want the role, purpose and contribution of TAs to be in your school?*

Let us clarify our terms. *Role* relates to the part(s) played by a TA in particular situation; this may lead you to create 'types' of TA role. The reason why these roles are needed is the *purpose*: put the needs of all the pupils in your school at the heart of change. Your decisions should lead to a direct or indirect impact on learning; in other words, there is an identifiable *contribution* made by TAs.

What you are seeking to achieve is to capture the uniqueness and essentialness of the TA role in your school. What is it your school could not do, or do as well, *without* your TAs? You need to situate this within the work of the school and even the wider community. Your TAs should be able to see their function within your school's overarching mission statement; where they fit in to the organisational machine. Doing this fulfils two vital purposes. Firstly, it very clearly privileges the TA role, and recognises their position, status and value. And secondly, it provides a foundation on which you and they can build a professional identity.

What is 'support'?

One way into thinking about the question above is to clarify how your staff use the term 'support' and what they understand it to mean. When school leaders, SENCOs, teachers and TAs ask themselves and each other the question, 'what do TAs do?', the responses are very often couched in terms of 'providing support': for teachers; for pupils with SEND; in the classroom; with teaching; with learning; with the curriculum.

The trouble is that even with further questioning, these notions of support are fuzzy and tell us surprisingly little about what TAs actually do and how it impacts on learning (Webster and Blatchford 2015; 2019). Consistency, therefore, becomes an issue. Conceptualisations of support and how these are operationalised can look different in different classrooms, even within the same school.

Your aim is to identify a clear vision to articulate what you want TAs to do in your setting to enhance teaching and learning, and improve pupil outcomes; in other words, pin down specific definitions of support. These should be limited to no more than three or four types of support; anything over this number and the fuzziness is likely to return. Consider too what it is you *do not* want TAs to do. There may be particular types of pedagogical support (i.e. subject expertise) that you need teachers to provide.

It is important you do not limit the discussion to the current ways of doing things, or to what you only *think* is possible under current, and perhaps, restricted conditions. Avoid the temptation to focus on 'outliers'; that is, how to overcome very specific circumstances or attitudes, which apply to only a few individuals, that may threaten the realisation of your vision. In short, this discussion is the time to set aside any limitations and imagine a whole new way of doing things. The material in the rest of this book can inform contributions to this discussion. Chapters 5 and 6 on TAs' deployment and practice are particularly relevant to generating ideas.

The bigger picture

Your vision for your TA workforce is likely to link or overlap with other areas of school improvement; for example, managing teachers' workload and narrowing the attainment gap between disadvantaged pupils and their peers. Making such connections is to be encouraged, as it reminds us that schools are 'ecosystems'.

As we have already mentioned, the work of the EEF and other organisations is useful in terms of helping schools to make informed decisions about interventions to raise attainment. But there is a danger that interventions, and the issues they are designed to address, are considered in relative isolation, as if apart from the ecosystem in which they sit. Tweaking or introducing a new initiative in one part of the system (e.g. a new catch-up reading scheme delivered by TAs) can have implications or opportunity costs elsewhere, for which we must account (e.g. pupils miss curriculum coverage; disjuncture between approaches to the teaching of reading may confuse pupils).

TAs are a big part of the current and lively conversation on effective, evidence-based interventions. What we learn from research is valuable in improving pupils' experiences and outcomes – but school leaders need to use it intelligently. They must critically engage with it, not follow it slavishly (Webster 2019). Research highlights options and possibilities; it does not provide certainties. You will need to weigh the evidence with your professional experience and your knowledge of your setting, staff and pupils in order to arrive at intelligent and well-rounded judgments.

In this book, we detail practical, workable strategies that have been successfully applied in 'real world' primary settings, and helped them realise *their* vision. There are two points of note here. Firstly, be mindful that importing a strategy from one setting into your own offers no guarantee of success. In the next chapter, we consider the role of implementation, and why you need to think hard about the processes that the schools featured in these pages have gone through in order to arrive at the solutions that work for them. Being curious about this is at least as important as your interest in the strategies themselves.

As we have mentioned already, this book focuses only on TAs, not on SEND provision more broadly. While this is necessary in order to make the guidance containable and not overly long, we are aware that in doing this, we risk atomising problems and solutions. It is important not to lose sight of how the role and function of TAs relates to SEND provision and other areas of thought and action, such as staff well-being, teachers' workload and their professional development requirements. Accordingly, we make every effort to relate specific points to these and other contexts and considerations. The second point to hold in mind, therefore, is that the schools whose work we reflect implemented MITA within *their* unique ecosystem. They were careful to integrate MITA into their school development plan alongside other areas of focus. You will need to consider throughout how MITA aligns with *your* strategic priorities in *your* setting.

As part of your initial action planning, you should consider the decision-making and actions you need to take that pertain: (i) directly to TAs; and (ii) to any other related areas, such as those we highlighted above. For example, you may decide to deploy TAs in ways that free teachers up to work with pupils with SEND. But if the impact of this is to be fully realised, you need to ensure your teachers receive specific up-to-date training on how to teach these pupils to maximum effect.

Planning for change

Schools are complex, dynamic environments in which to successfully implement change on the scale outlined in this book. Factor in changes that involve people, their contracts, the fundamentals of their role and purpose, their professional identities, and the emotions discussing this is likely to provoke, and you have a particularly knotty problem on your hands.

Clearly, it is not our intention to discourage you at such an early stage, but we know from the many schools we have worked with that it is not uncommon for at least some TAs to experience some anxiety (see Chapter 3). It is important, therefore, for school leaders to be upfront with staff right from the start. These schools tell us that while MITA is challenging, like anything that requires time and effort, the rewards are unequivocally worth it.

It is useful to consider Timothy Knoster's advice (Knoster et al. 2000) about understanding the essential components of systemic organisational reform. His model of managing complex change suggests that when the components of vision, skills, incentives, resources and an action plan are all in place, achieving the desired change is far more likely. However, if any one of the five components is missing, the change process is liable to incur problems. For example, without a vision, there is confusion; without resources, there is frustration; without incentives, you encounter resistance; and without an action plan, you are likely to experience false starts or remain on the treadmill.

We will address skills specifically in Chapters 6 and 7, but as a good example of the anxiety that Knoster says the lack of skills can produce, it is worth considering whether your TAs have experience of or the aptitude for being part of professional conversations with members of SLT. We mention this because we have found that TAs can interpret discussions and comments about their practice as personal criticism. At least one explanation for this is that, compared with teachers, TAs are less accustomed to participating in processes of performance management and professional development. A helpful precondition of the work ahead, therefore, is to ensure your TAs are able and ready to play a full and active part in a dialogue about their role. One way we have seen school leaders lay the ground for this is to set TAs the task of developing their own set of professional standards (e.g. conduct, punctuality, etc.). It is worth adding that all members of SLT need to be skilled in leading professional conversations.

As you work through the chapters of this book, we recommend you and your SLT begin to draft a logic model. A logic model can help you to identify and tabulate the active ingredients of an intervention. You can capture a logic model on a single side of A4, by zeroing in on the key concepts, areas of action and outcomes.[1] The logic model can then be used to populate a more detailed action plan. You may have a preferred method or framework you use for action planning, but for those in need of a starting point, you can download a template from our website.

Towards implementation

Having developed your vision and started to sketch out a plan for achieving it, you must use every possible means and opportunity to regularly communicate the vision and strategies. This is the fourth step on Kotter's path to implementing successful change. It is important to think of this phase of implementation as looking for consent, rather than approval. It goes without saying that you want to bring your staff with you, not drag them along. You want them to be receptive to what MITA offers and involves, and be ready to go on the journey. All of your staff should be able to agree to being open and willing to trust the MITA process and your handling of it – even if some individuals may struggle to visualise what it entails for them or have reservations about whether it will succeed.

Securing the buy-in of a critical mass of your workforce is very likely to require repeated effort. As your journey proceeds, be sure to look over your shoulder at regular intervals. Who is finding the going tricky? Who needs encouragement to carry on? Who is still stood on the start line, claiming they did not hear the starting pistol? What do they need to hear from you to nudge them along?

Schools undertaking the MITA programme use their guiding coalitions to test and model new strategies. These teams are supported in their actions by senior leaders who empower their staff to challenge and improve existing ways of doing things and to take risks. Removing obstacles that could undermine change is important. Your staff should not be held back by thinking that leads them to test safe strategies with a high chance of success. To empower action (Kotter's fifth step), you must ensure that all outcomes of developmental work – that is, whether a trial has worked – have equal value. It is as important to know what does not work and why, as it is to know what works successfully and the conditions for success.

Your group of teachers and TAs that pilot strategies should be encouraged to share their learning with colleagues. Kotter refers to 'generating short-term wins' (step 6) that build school-wide support for change. That ideas are generated and shared organically through a peer-led process that avoids a sense of top-down imposition and is likely to encourage the participation of more resistant colleagues. Consolidating gains and producing more change (step 7) not only embeds ideas and encourages new ones, but also helps transform the culture of the school. This is essential for institutionalising a positive 'change culture' (step 8), which ensures staff have the right dispositions needed to engage with the continuous drive for school improvement.

In the next chapter, we will focus on the process of implementation. We will look at how some of the most successful schools we have worked with have achieved change and improved classroom processes and pupils' experiences and outcomes. In doing so, we intend to provide inspiration as well as a workable, relatable model to help you bring *your* vision to life.

Note

1 You can download a logic model (or implementation plan) template, and some worked examples from other school-based projects, at https://educationendowmentfoundation.org.uk/tools/guidance-reports/a-schools-guide-to-implementation/

Chapter 3

Implementation journeys
The most important chapter of this book

'Vision without implementation is hallucination'.

Thomas Edison

What is implementation and why is it important?

We briefly discussed the role and significance of implementation in Chapter 1, but here we explore this topic in more detail than we have in any of our previous writing. You may be tempted to skip to the following chapter in which we outline the next step of the MITA process, but taking the time now to consider *how* you are going to realise your vision reflects one of the single most important lessons we have learned from our work with schools over many years. Spending time at this preparatory stage, thinking about how you bring this programme of work into your setting, predict and limit probable hitches, and give it the best possible chance of success, may save you a lot of time and trouble in the long run.

Implementation is the groundwork one does ahead of a project – from planting a vegetable bed in your garden, to building a skyscraper – and it is especially relevant to initiatives like MITA that affect whole organisations. As the leading educationalist and former Chief Executive of the EEF, Sir Kevan Collins, is quoted as saying, 'implementation isn't sexy' (Sharples 2019). But it is a prerequisite for success. As the old adage goes: fail to prepare, and prepare to fail.

External pressures, busy calendars and the pace of life in school can result in leaders sometimes sidestepping the foundational work, or lulling themselves into thinking that one staff briefing is sufficient to communicate the objectives and methods. They push things through at speed, overlook the complexity of what they are trying to achieve, or perhaps assume every member of staff is on board from the get-go. You may be able to think of an example from your own experience, where a more careful preparation would have avoided a particular hurdle that undermined or even upended the whole venture. Never lose sight of the reason we do anything in school: to benefit, directly or indirectly, the pupils. It is they who miss out (unknowingly) when our well-intentioned efforts blow up on the launchpad.

To be fair to school leaders, competing priorities, the pace of change, and the burden of accountability that often comes with it, can and do work against good implementation. If you are under pressure to show an improvement in reading scores in Key Stage 1 within half a term, for example, you are unlikely to have the luxury of time to meticulously consider all the available options and the possible consequences, or to change course if your first attempt is not working out as planned. In such circumstances, you may be tempted to look for a promising, 'oven-ready' package, press it into action in double-quick time, and deal with any problems that may arise along the way.

In the end, the promise of MITA – and almost any other educational innovation – is realised through not only *what* schools do, but *how* they do it. What makes the difference with MITA is how it manifests itself in the day-to-day work of your staff and how you lead and manage change.

Projects initiated with the best of intentions can fizzle out. We have seen this with schools that begin MITA, only to see it splutter to a halt just yards from the start line. Oftentimes the cause is linked to implementation relying too much on instinct, or work proceeded on the basis of incorrect assumptions or incomplete information. No-one wants to feel that their time has been wasted, and there is a particular risk here with MITA. A failed attempt at making a concerted effort to realise and maximise the untapped potential of TAs in your school could leave them disillusioned, as well as reinforce any belief that might already exist that they are undervalued.

If schools are about anything, it is learning: to continuously change in order to be more effective, so that their pupils can achieve and reach their potential. Implementation is what schools do to improve. We think, as organisations, schools ought to reflect the attributes they want to nurture in children: trying new things; reflecting on those experiences; and habituating the practices that work best. These are not just characteristics of an effective learning mindset; they are also fundamental to a healthy implementation mindset.

Aligning the 'what' with the 'how'

On the basis of current research, we can have a relatively high level of confidence in *what* it is schools ought to do, and ought not to do, in order to maximise the impact of TAs. When schools align their decision-making and practice with recommendations based on the best available evidence, the negative results of the DISS project are sufficiently mitigated, and the probability of improved outcomes for pupils increases (Maxwell et al. 2019).

Our understanding of 'what works' in terms of deploying and preparing TAs is, we believe, sufficiently advanced for us to switch at least some of the research effort elsewhere. As our colleague in the US, Michael Giangreco (2021) notes, further research on the clarification of the TA role, training, planning time with teachers and supervision is, and will remain, important. But the relative narrowness and frequency with which the research community fixates on this small set of issues should not distract us from other important research questions on this topic. For Giangreco, the most overlooked and under-explored issue relates to models of inclusion that comprise effective alternatives to the overreliance on TAs. To this we can add questions about the school-level processes needed to successfully operationalise evidence-based practices concerning TAs. In other words, *how* to do the 'what'.

Perhaps because the operative word in 'what works' is 'what', attention tends to be directed at tangible, predefined inputs that can be imported, ideally seamlessly, into a particular context. The potential outcomes of a specified intervention can be seductive. 'Independent evaluations of "Programme X" show that disadvantaged pupils make three months of additional progress. If we start running it in our school, great things will follow!' It does not matter how firmly you believe in the evidence of its impact,

Programme X is unlikely to make a difference to disadvantaged pupils in your setting *unless* you attend to and replicate the processes by which successful schools introduced, implemented and embedded it.

Another reason why 'what to do' tends to trump 'how to do it', at least in the case of the England, is because our accountability system does not reward good implementation. School leaders are accustomed to being judged on the impact of their decision-making on academic outcomes – and good implementation without good outcomes counts for little. This pressurised environment also nudges school leaders toward prescriptive methods; that is, strategies and approaches that can be implemented by following a straightforward, tightly defined set of instructions. A good example is the pre-packaged, ready-to-go TA-led structured interventions we mentioned in Chapter 1. Implementation tends to be more straightforward when it comes to introducing these because they can be slotted in without requiring too many changes to existing practices and routines.

Schools can be more reluctant to engage with initiatives where implementation is protracted and the processes somewhat abstract; in other words, where applying the operating instructions requires greater amounts of interpretation and measured judgment. A whole-school approach to improving the use of TAs exhibits these features, and implies extensive, and potentially disruptive, change. Yet, an emergent theme from the latest research suggests that when it comes to the effective use of TAs throughout the school, rolling up your sleeves and engaging with these crunchy problems is essential to capitalising on the promises of 'what works'.

Bringing coherence to the MITA process

Before we begin to describe and demystify the implementation process as it relates to MITA, let us say something about the development and status of our approach.

For several years now, we have been integrating learning from the research and literature on implementation science and improvement science into what we believe is a well-honed and empirically strong, best-practice model for making the best use of TAs. Our approach can be seen as part of the wider and rapidly evolving field of implementation in educational settings – the constituent elements of which are developing at different rates. For example, the robustness of our store of knowledge on training and professional development is relatively stronger than on implementation climate, which so far has not been as extensively studied (Sharples, Albers and Fraser 2019).

For the purposes of this book, our strategy has been to do as much of the heavy lifting as possible, by weaving the salient and relevant aspects from the implementation world into the MITA process. Space does not allow for a more expansive discussion of the implementation discipline, so we recommend that you take a look at some of the accessible and actionable guidance and resources[1], and consider them in conjunction with this book.

What the (limited) evidence tells us

The evaluations of large-scale campaigns to roll out the EEF's *Making Best Use of Teaching Assistants* guidance in schools across Yorkshire and Lincolnshire[2] found that the effect of the context and characteristics of the school and their leaders were perceived to be important for effective implementation (Maxwell et al. 2019). Successful implementation was associated with schools where: senior leaders were committed, capable, enthusiastic and understood the implications of changes at the school and classroom level; time was allocated to implementing change and for staff to engage in associated activity (e.g. ensuring part-time staff could participate); and there was a clear process for implementation. However, schools had variable, often weak, capacity across these attributes.

Of equal importance in the success of MITA is fidelity: how faithfully you stick to its key principles and follow its main steps. A related concept to fidelity is that of compliance: the extent to which you do what it is a programme specifies or directs you to do. It is perfectly possible for a school to be highly compliant with an intervention, but for it to make little or no difference to pupil outcomes. For instance, the staff could attend a professional learning session – which ticks a compliance box – but not be attentive. Equally, the delivery of the training, and even the training itself, might be poor.

What we want to draw attention to throughout this book is a set of processes that weave in and through, between and around the good practice exemplars stemming from the WPR model. Coherence is a necessary condition for introducing, implementing and sustaining the organisation-wide changes we cover in this book.

Implementation journeys

As we indicated earlier, a key motivation for writing this book was to address the question raised by school leaders about how to operationalise MITA. The data we require to answer this question are best obtained from dedicated inquires that prioritise the implementation process and focus on bringing to light the experiences of schools claiming some success in relation to this. Over the years, we have developed some good relationships with a number of schools that have expressed a keenness to share their experiences and the practices they felt were making a difference in their settings.

With the preparation of this book in mind, we conducted a small study involving schools across England that took part in regional iterations of the MITA programme, carried out between 2017 and 2019. We called this project 'MITA Journeys'. On the basis of ongoing notes of MITA leadership training sessions, discussions and visits, which captured schools' experiences of implementing MITA, we identified a group of primary schools that we felt were uniquely positioned to offer detailed insight into the steps required to successfully instigate and implement a programme of whole school change concerning the use of TAs. As the majority of schools that undertake MITA are primary schools, we decided to focus the MITA Journeys project and this book on this specific phase.

Our implementation inquiry necessarily required a purposive sampling strategy[3]; we targeted schools that demonstrated particularly high levels of commitment to MITA. We were delighted that several dozen schools expressed an interest in sharing their journeys, but unfortunately we could not involve them all. From this group, we selected five primary schools to participate in the project. We visited the schools and met with the leadership team, and groups of TAs and teachers to conduct in-depth, semi-structured interviews about their respective experiences of implementing MITA.

Because implementation is essentially about leadership, this chapter prioritises the experiences, reflections and voices of school leaders. The direct quotations presented in this chapter are drawn from our interviews with school leaders, while the thoughts and views of TAs and teachers feature more prominently in Chapters 5, 6 and 7. We found, when analysing the interview data, that TAs and teachers corroborated much of what school leaders told us. As you progress through the book, you will notice that there is a pleasing degree of consistency between the quotations from leaders, TAs and teachers from the same setting.

We have structured our presentation of findings using Kotter's change model, which we introduced in the previous chapter. Headteachers, senior leaders and SENCOs were familiar with this framework, as we refer to it in the MITA strategy sessions. It provides a flexible framework for drilling down and drawing out data on the implementation of both the MITA programme's components and their overall coherence. We have used a broader categorisation developed by Kotter himself, which clusters the eight steps into three phases of implementation:

- Phase 1. Creating a climate for change (steps 1, 2 and 3)
- Phase 2. Engaging and enabling staff (steps 4, 5 and 6)
- Phase 3. Implementing and sustaining change (steps 7 and 8)

Introducing the MITA Journeys schools

Before going any further, let us introduce the MITA Journeys schools by presenting their key characteristics in Table 3.1. The columns furthest right indicate the number of TAs and teachers on staff (headcount) and how many of each took part in the interviews. We interviewed 26 TAs and 21 teachers, plus the headteacher and one other senior leader per school.

Phase I. Creating a climate for change

Step I. Establish a case for change

The first phase of Kotter's model marks out the foundations of good implementation, starting with a clear rationale and defining purpose for action. At the first MITA strategy session for school leaders, we made the case for change to schools in much the same way we did in Chapter 1. In some settings, including several of the MITA Journeys schools, a

Table 3.1 The MITA Journeys schools

School name	Region	Form entry	Pupils on roll	TAs		Teachers	
				Headcount	Interview	Headcount	Interview
Alver Valley	Hampshire	2	314	22	4	18	4
Crestwood	West Midlands	1	208	14	12	9	8
Cuddington Croft	Surrey	2	487	24	2	21	2
Laureate	Suffolk	1	265	17	6	15	5
Shirley Manor	Yorkshire	1	210	17	2	9	2

Note: Headcounts include pupils and staff in nursery (where applicable). All pupil and staff headcount data were collected in the summer term 2017 culture had been normalised, whereby TAs were employed and deployed in order to accommodate pupils with SEND. However, little or no thought had been given to communicating the purpose of the role, clarifying expectations, or identifying and supporting individual's professional learning needs.

> The answer was to put a body with a child, even if that body was somebody who hadn't been trained.
>
> Alver Valley

> Historically, there was an extent to which TAs, and especially newly appointed TAs, were just thrown in and left to get on with it.
>
> Laureate

Schools had grown sizeable TA workforces, but at the same time the management of TAs had been allowed to drift. Without clear direction, TAs had constructed their own professional identity and defining practices. It was common to hear of TAs 'over-nurturing' or 'over-supporting' pupils, but school leaders attributed this to a failure of leadership, and not a fault of TAs.

In addition to the lack of role clarity and purpose, school leaders identified TAs' exclusion from processes, such as performance management and training, as contributory factors to disenfranchisement, and feelings of anxiety and being undervalued. Leaders of MITA Journeys schools recognised the cultural impact of this situation, which in turn justified action.

> [TAs] had not really been engaged in any of the decisions about them... Nobody really talked to them about what they needed to be doing in the classroom.
>
> Alver Valley

> ...over half of our staff are TAs and [if] they're not happy, that has a massive impact on the feel of the school.
>
> Crestwood

School leaders applied their concern over the longstanding injustice towards TAs, and the evolution of inconsistent and ineffective practices (both unintentional) to imbue a sense of urgency. Schools saw MITA as an opportunity to reinvigorate their TA workforce. In the previous chapter, we talked about capturing the uniqueness and essentialness of the TA role. We found that, as part of their vision-setting phase, school leaders tended to ask staff to answer questions like: 'Why are TAs fundamental to improving the learning and life chances of pupils at our school?; and 'What is great about being a TA at our school?'

Step 2. Create a guiding coalition

Having made a compelling case for challenging the status quo regarding the use of TAs, we encouraged schools to form a development team to help steer planning and decision-making. Teams were composed of the headteacher, another senior leader or the SENCO, and one or two teachers and TAs from each Key Stage and (where applicable) the early years. Leaders brought on board individuals they felt had a strategic usefulness, ensuring as many voices as possible were represented, but being mindful not to let the team become so populous that things became impractical. TAs who carried influence in the wider TA team acted as mediators. Some headteachers brought 'the sceptics' and those with 'challenging opinions' inside the process.

> We got some of the 'resisters' on board... to show them that they could have an influence on the change... As we've gone along, so their voice is being heard.
>
> Shirley Manor

Importantly, MITA Journeys schools described using their team to ensure that TAs had some ownership of the process. As the Headteacher of Shirley Manor put it, it was important for leaders to demonstrate that MITA 'wasn't being done *to* them; it was being done *with* them'.

Step 3. Develop a clear vision

In the previous chapter, we cited Knoster's point that in the absence of a well specified path toward a clearly defined vision, schools are at risk of going around in circles. We pressed home the importance of developing a clear vision, and set it as a gap task following our first strategic leadership session.

Given the aforementioned concerns about TAs 'over-supporting' pupils, it is not surprising that almost every school that engages with MITA sets the development of pupil independence as a central outcome that they want to achieve. What emerged strongly from the interviews with leaders in the MITA Journeys schools was the value they placed on the essentialness of vision-setting to the realisation of this aim. They described an initial process of characterising elements of the vision in terms of what it would look like in the classroom. We referred to this process of reverse engineering in Chapter 2 as 'starting with the end in mind'.

> When we set the vision, it was very much focused on pupil independence. We spent a long-time unpicking, what is it we wanted to achieve, why is it important, what's it going to look like in two years' time, and then worked backwards.
>
> Laureate

Thereon, defining and refining the vision was, for many schools, an iterative process, which involved input from staff. Iterations of the vision were stress-tested in regular meetings. Several leaders in MITA Journeys schools talked about the conscious and repeated effort required to anchor actions to a clear vision, which had to be kept 'front and centre' of the school's development priorities.

> Right from the word go, it was part of the school improvement plan... You've got to be clear about your vision, what ethos you want, and where your end goal is... We had to keep coming back to: 'Stop. What is our ethos and vision for the school? Where do we want our children to be?'
>
> Alver Valley

School leaders concluded that the vision-setting phase of the MITA process was time-consuming, but essential. A key message they had for other leaders was to be realistic about, and not compromise on, the time commitment required to develop a clear vision, which can be intuitively understood and shared across the school. This fitted with the many comments we had about MITA not being 'a quick fix'.

Phase 2. Engaging and enabling staff

Step 4. Communicate the vision

The second phase of implementation segues from planning to action. This begins with taking the vision to the staff team and helping them to visualise what it will mean for them in their everyday practice.

There was variation in the way MITA was initially received by teachers and TAs. For example, in three of the MITA Journeys schools, the TAs, with one or two exceptions, were described as 'buzzing' and 'immediately energised' by the launch meetings. At the other schools, however, news of the project sparked anxiety – especially in terms of job security.

> TAs were very worried and scared as to what it would entail.
>
> Shirley Manor

> TAs initially thought this is a way of rationalising them.
>
> Crestwood

Despite the mixed responses from TAs, the teachers were broadly consistent in their reactions to MITA. They were ambivalent and less engaged. Again, what happened in the MITA Journeys schools was reflective of moods and reactions in many other schools that undertake the programme.

> We launched it with the teachers, and it really fell on almost deaf ears... I think they also thought, it either doesn't affect me because it's about TAs; or, are [senior leaders] going to make us do more work?
>
> Alver Valley

It is rare that each and every member of staff accepts and understands a new initiative the first time they hear about it. Beyond this though, school leaders attributed the initial lack of vision clarity to the failure to grab everyone's attention at the outset. On reflection, they also speculated whether this vagueness was an artefact of wanting to avoid the appearance of diktat. It is possible that in making the process collaborative, confusion was unintentionally introduced. A vacuum opened in which teachers and TAs constructed their own interpretations of what MITA was and what it would mean for them. Referring directly to Kotter's model, the Headteacher at Alver Valley described how the first attempt to launch MITA necessitated returning to previous steps.

> We thought we were at step four, and I thought: 'We're going to have to go again. There's something that's not right. We're not getting across to them.'... We had to launch it about two or three times, and take on their anxieties.
>
> Alver Valley

Step 5. Empowering people to act on the vision

GENERATING AND SECURING STAFF BUY-IN

Assuaging anxieties about what involvement in MITA meant was a precondition of efforts to empower staff to act on the vision. Leaders listened to TAs' and teachers' concerns and reinforced what MITA was, and was not, designed to achieve. This was recognised as an important part of securing consent and support.

> In the early days, it was just reassuring people that there isn't an ulterior motive [making redundancies]… It came out that there were some misconceptions and misunderstandings. I had meetings with small groups of people just to try and reassure.
>
> Crestwood

The persistent, but carefully handled messaging to TAs, was a 'big turning point' at Crestwood. At Alver Valley, the leadership team identified how 'stresses outside of school' prevented TAs from engaging with MITA, and provided individualised personal support to help them at work.

We learned that in some schools, the TAs on the development team became effective mediators between the leadership team and the rest of the TA workforce, providing support and relaying information on a peer-to-peer level in order to bring their colleagues on board.

For the teachers, bringing them onside was not just about providing reassurances that their workload would not increase, but being explicit about what MITA looked like in their day-to-day practice.

> It's almost a shift in mindset. We talked a lot about marking and feedback… if you skill up your TA and work in partnership with them, they can do some of that marking and feedback for you, in the lesson. Therefore, you've got maybe six fewer books to mark. Actually, that's freeing up your time… TAs are instrumental in helping you achieve those targets for your children.
>
> Cuddington Croft

Another effective strategy for securing buy-in from staff was to highlight how MITA integrated with other initiatives. At Alver Valley, the SLT identified and reinforced a 'golden thread' in order to forge linkages between the element of MITA designed to foster pupils' independence with strands of an existing initiative aimed at developing children's dispositions for learning, including independence and resilience. Shirley Manor did similar, by using MITA to build on recent work on growth mindset: 'It just added nicely and flowed on from that'. In a number of schools, we found that elements of MITA were absorbed in the feedback and marking policy. Consistent with what we said in the previous chapter, the key point is that schools made the effort to ensure that their TAs could see themselves reflected in an overarching mission.

TRIALLING NEW APPROACHES AND SKILLING-UP TAS

In order to alleviate concerns about what MITA would look like in the classroom (and secure buy-in), school leaders took early action to give elements of their vision tangible form. We encouraged schools to ask teacher and TA pairs on the development team to conduct some small-scale trials of new approaches.

> The Key Stage 2 pair worked on what preparation meetings might look like and how to make best use of those... The Early Years pair focused on having a teacher–TA agreement.[4]
>
> Laureate

School leaders described how, in this phase of implementation, TAs expressed their training needs and the areas in which they needed support. In many schools, this led to the creation of regular training and development sessions for TAs, which built on the Maximising the Practice of Teaching Assistants (MPTA) component of the programme.

Step 6. Create short-term wins

The advantage of early wins is not cynical short-termism, but a vital part of building school-wide support and providing the evidence to motivate any remaining uncertain or resistant colleagues. Schools reported that the process of obtaining buy-in from every teacher and TA was enhanced by quick and decisive action to address a particular common and persistent practical problem: having little or no time to meet together outside of lessons. The comments below from MITA Journeys schools were indicative of what we hear from other schools that undertake the programme.

> Time for communication came out strongly between both camps as being a key problem. So we put it in place; now they've got a designated time together.
>
> Shirley Manor

> Something that we very quickly started with was the preparedness time, and we got that launched very quickly.
>
> Laureate

We will focus on the issue of preparedness in Chapter 7, but it is worth mentioning two popular approaches to creating liaison time exemplified by MITA Journeys schools: (i) using assembly time; and (ii) offering flexible working or time off in lieu to TAs.

> We [senior leaders] took on an extra responsibility to run celebration assembly, which tends to be the longest one of the week.
>
> Cuddington Croft

> As preparedness meetings are mostly happening at lunchtimes or before school, TAs can go half an hour earlier one day that week. That's something I thought we might have had a bit of resistance around, but we haven't had any quibbles from teachers about losing TA classroom support time.
>
> Laureate

This comment from the Headteacher at Laureate reveals the importance of not losing support once it has been gained. Here then, it is important to be clear about trade-offs. In this case, teachers remained onside because the loss of some TA support time in the classroom was sufficiently offset by the benefit of having liaison time. In many schools, we found that the effect of providing liaison time had the effect of TAs feeling more included in school life.

> [Meetings with teachers make TAs] feel more included. It gives them an idea of the bigger picture... Another thing that has really helped is involving the TAs in the pupil progress meetings
>
> Crestwood

The MPTA training for TAs on effective scaffolding was also referred to by leaders as providing an early win. MPTA gave TAs practical and immediately implementable strategies to integrate into their classroom practice, and a foundation on which to build and embed change.

Phase 3. Implementing and sustaining change

Step 7. Consolidate and build on gains

The final phase on implementation of Kotter's model concerns how organisations concretise new processes and practices. This was the phase that the schools were at, two years into the MITA process. By this juncture, school leaders were able to articulate forms of impact. First and foremost, they spoke about the impact on their TAs. These comments from MITA Journeys schools were illustrative of what we heard from schools at the final regional strategy sessions.

> I think it has definitely raised their professional profile.
>
> Alver Valley

> I feel like they're more empowered. I feel like they're more confident... So much more valued.
>
> Cuddington Croft

At the classroom level, leaders reported more purposeful deployment of TAs by teachers and the emergence of teaching teams or partnerships (see Chapter 5). This was in contrast to previous practice, where the roles and actions of teachers and TAs in lessons were uncoordinated. Again, the evidence from MITA Journeys schools reflects changes in other schools that undertake the programme.

> Teachers have genuinely rethought their own deployment as well as their deployment of their TAs and are making sure that all pupils, especially the most disadvantaged pupils have as much access to the teacher as possible.
>
> Laureate

Teachers had more confidence in TAs' capabilities and this had created capacity and eased workload. The realisation of these benefits helped allay teachers' earlier concerns (see step 5).

It's generated a bit of extra capacity... Now we have a lot more TAs setting up and looking after a class, covering for short periods of time.

Alver Valley

TAs are marking [pupils' work in lessons], so marking's reduced for the teachers. [Teachers] are starting to see that then impacts on the work they do in class and it makes it easier for them.

Shirley Manor

Perhaps the most persuasive area of impact that leaders felt would maintain momentum was in relation to pupil outcomes. It is important to note that it is difficult to prove causation here, but on the basis of their own observations and evidence-gathering, school leaders were confident that positive effects were materialising.

Our Ofsted report makes a really strong nod to the independence skills of the children.

Laureate

We're seeing that the progress, especially of our SEND children, is really, really coming through.

Shirley Manor

Step 8. Institutionalise the change

School leaders were highly motivated to capitalise on and sustain the improvements they had identified in their settings. As we noted above (step 6), schools used the training for TAs on scaffolding learning (see Chapter 6) to monitor and embed effective new practices. We provided guidance for leaders on how to reinforce and sustain this training.

Everyone, on their performance management, has got a MITA project target.

Alver Valley

All of the TAs now have got one appraisal target on the scaffolding framework.

Cuddington Croft

Given the inevitability of staff turnover, leaders in the MITA Journeys schools planned to ensure consistent levels of institutional knowledge by including the scaffolding training in induction programmes and using it as the basis for on-going professional development programmes for TAs.

A final theme to emerge concerned the need to resist slipping back to ineffective practices. School leaders had expressed this previously in comments at the final strategy session at the end of the previous school year. A year later, leaders of the MITA Journeys schools were again talking about 'relaunching' the project at the start of the forthcoming school year 'so we don't lose the impact or lose the momentum'.

If you're not careful, you do it and it's all looking like it's all going well, then you take your eye off it and it'll fall.

Shirley Manor

We're keeping MITA very high profile, because you lose it otherwise... it's one of those things that can get lost in the shuffle of a busy school

Laureate

We don't want to lose the momentum... we can't go back to [TAs] sharpening pencils in the corner.

Cuddington Croft

The reason why we're carrying on is because we could never revert back to how it was before, and we think we can still get more out of it.

Crestwood

Summary of findings from the MITA Journeys study

A key purpose of this chapter is to focus attention on the implementation of MITA in a way that no other authors on this topic (including us) have previously achieved. The need to do so is justified not just by the gap in the literature, but through our years of experiences of working with schools, which has revealed that leaders' understanding and acceptance of our evidence-based guidance is not matched with knowledge and confidence about how to act on it. Here, then, we have provided fresh insight into how primary school leaders have managed organisational change within the context of MITA. While our sample of schools is small and selective, it is striking that the lessons school leaders shared, the challenges they faced, the barriers overcome, and the obstacles remaining and ahead, are familiar to almost every school that undertakes MITA. While we cannot claim that our study sample is representative, their experiences certainly are. Let us summarise several key themes of the implementation journeys our five schools have taken.

Firstly, leaders described a clear and urgent need for undertaking MITA in the first place, which related to correcting the oversight of a previous administration: the TA workforce had expanded, but without any strategic purpose. This unintentional drift meant TAs were unclear about their role, and this was exhibited in the kinds of ineffective practices found in the DISS project (e.g. over-supporting). Schools set a new vision for TAs centred on improving pupil independence. The high levels of commitment showed to the MITA programme were indicative of leaders taking responsibility for the situation into which the school had drifted.

Secondly, the leaders gave themselves permission to pace the implementation of MITA, and they prioritised the involvement of staff from the outset. This was particularly significant for TAs, who were drawn into and consulted on processes from which they had hitherto been excluded. Taking a collaborative approach provided a partial early gain, but it also aroused suspicion. The years of austerity put an unwanted inflection on MITA, with TAs fearing job cuts. Teachers, meanwhile, were wary of increased workload. It was notable that school leaders took time and effort to alleviate staff's anxieties and persuade them of the benefits of MITA. To use our analogy of a journey, this phase of implementation was about getting everybody on the bus. Leaders' visibility and high level of effort seem significant here, as it is likely to have tacitly communicated the importance of MITA, and by definition, TAs. Strategies, such as tasking members of the development team with trialling solutions to the issues most salient to them (e.g. preparedness), and including TAs in processes that previously only involved teachers (e.g. pupil progress meetings), reinforced principles of consent, collaboration and ownership of the process. Involvement in processes and the visible impact of early gains helped dial down the threat and allowed leaders to secure the buy-in of a critical mass of the workforce.

Finally, the early gains paid off in terms of improvements to TAs' self-confidence, motivation and sense of value. Teachers were persuaded by seeing tangible benefits of better preparation and deployment of TAs to themselves and their teaching. Two years into the MITA process, none of the school leaders said their journey was complete. Entering the final phase of implementation (implementing and sustaining change), they were clear that going forward, the challenge was to maintain momentum and fully embed new processes into existing systems (e.g. staff induction; performance management) and the life and culture of the school. Vigilance was required in order to avoid complacency or slipping back to old practices.

Chapter summary

We have been upfront in terms of characterising this chapter as the most important one in this book. We recognise that matters of implementation can be somewhat abstract, and therefore harder to engage with. Also, as we noted, there are no accolades in our accountability system for good implementation. This perhaps explains why school leaders are less intuitively drawn to implementation in and of itself. However, we think we can make a strong case for its value by bringing implementation to life in the context of something school leader are intrinsically motivated by – in this case, making the best use of TAs.

Our aim in this chapter has been to exemplify some core principles and processes of change management, and to demonstrate the impact of interleaving implementation techniques into the MITA process. In the following chapters of this book, we will shift our focus from the 'how' to the 'what'. In doing so, we will revisit our MITA Journeys schools and look in detail at the approaches they introduced to improve the deployment, practice and preparedness of TAs.

One final point to make. Given what we have said about the abstract nature of implementation, you may find that, having worked your way through the rest of this book and having learned more about 'what works' regarding TAs, there is value in rereading this chapter. This will reinforce the coherence and interrelatedness of our evidence-based strategies and the process of mobilising them in your setting.

Notes

1 A good starting point for this is the guidance and materials produced by the EEF, which are available at https://educationendowmentfoundation.org.uk/tools/guidance-reports/a-schools-guide-to-implementation/.

The UK Implementation Society aims to 'build capacity and expertise for more effective, evidence-informed implementation of services for people and communities', and is a good source of resources, expertise, and support on implementation: https://www.ukimplementation.org.uk/about. Finally, the Normalization Process Theory website carries a free interactive toolkit to help think critically through implementation and integration issues and rate your readiness and progress. It was developed for use in health care settings, but the 16 questions are just as applicable to schools: http://www.normalizationprocess.org/npt-toolkit/.

2 Interviews with members of the regional campaign delivery team (30 in total), school-based project leads (15), and interviews with school leaders, teachers and TAs in 16 participating schools.

3 *A note on potential bias.* One of the trade-offs in using a purposive sample is that participants can be biased when reporting on their own experiences. Additionally, they may have been influenced, consciously or unconsciously, by the fact that they were providing evidence to the MITA team; they may, therefore, have held back criticisms that they would have reported to an independent researcher. It is also important to note the bias that the authors, as researchers and developers, may introduce. Again, they may unconsciously emphasise positive experiences, and pay comparatively less attention to less favourable experiences, on the basis that the latter might reveal unintended consequences of the developmental work in which much professional time had been invested. We are, however, confident that the portrayal of MITA in this book is fair and balanced.

4 A checklist of roles a TA might take at during a lesson. For more on the teacher–TA agreement, see Chapter 5.

Chapter 4

Reviewing current practice

Why conduct an audit?

Every school leader values their TA workforce. But how much do you know about how the decisions you take regarding TAs impacts on practice in the classroom? Our extensive research into the use and impact of TAs has shown the inadvertent effects of TA support are inextricably linked to the decisions made about TAs' deployment and preparation. This is an important point. It means that the best predictors of how effective TAs are in classrooms are not the decisions and actions that they take, but the decisions and actions made by school leaders.

It is worth adding that these strategic decisions – and the gaps created when decisions are not taken – provide the framework and legitimacy for decisions at the classroom level taken (or not) by teachers. This too is an important point, and consistent with what we know about the effects of leaders 'setting the weather' in their school.[1]

A stark message from the DISS project was the disjuncture that can exist between the perceptions held by school leaders and what happens in the classroom. The impressions school leaders and teachers had about the effectiveness of TAs were at variance with the objective measures of TA impact we collected in the study. In short, what school leaders *believed* to be effective ways of using TAs, were in fact – pedagogically speaking – doing more harm than good.

Verifying what you think you know is one of the clearest justifications for an audit. Another is being sure that before you implement any kind of change, you have a full understanding of the situation with which you are engaging. In the case of MITA, this amounts to obtaining a detailed picture of how TAs are currently deployed and prepared in your school, and of the nature and quality of their interactions with pupils.

An audit is also useful for identifying what your school is doing well and the areas where development is needed. This helps leaders to locate and share existing best practice across the school, and to be precise about where improvements are needed, so that resources can be appropriately targeted. Also, the results can act as a baseline against which you can evaluate change at a later date, using the same processes. This chapter covers the auditing process and provides you with the tools to undertake an evaluation of current practice in your setting.

Together with your vision, the audit is the starting point for your MITA journey. It is an early opportunity for you to capture the valuable contribution TAs make to teaching and learning, and to school life generally. Our audit is designed to support a process by which leadership teams can make more informed decisions about TA deployment, practice and preparation, which will allow TAs to thrive in their role, and contribute to improved outcomes for pupils.

Aims of the audit

Before we get to the audit itself, it is helpful to specify what the audit is designed to achieve – and also what it is not.

You should aim to collect data that provide both an objective and subjective picture of current practice. As we have noted, it is important to get a clear sense of the extent to which: (i) what you *think* is happening in classrooms across the school matches the reality; and (ii) your perceptions of what is happening (and its effects) are shared by your staff. A further point to consider, therefore, is how different parts of the audit link together. As you will see, our process helps you to obtain a picture of TA deployment and practice moving from the broad school level, through the classroom level, right down to the fine detail of the pupil experience.

As we explained in the Introduction, TAs are often handed the duty of planning, delivering and assessing structured interventions. It is worth supplementing this audit with a parallel review of the delivery and impact of intervention programmes. We will not dwell further on auditing TA-led interventions here, but we will revisit this in Chapter 8.

Given the well-established link between TA deployment and processes of inclusion for pupils with SEND, decisions about TAs often interact with decisions about SEND, and vice versa. There is value in aligning this audit with a broader review of SEND provision. Whole School SEND have produced a review guide to support this process, which you can download for free via the SEND Gateway, at www.sendgateway.org.uk.

We want to be very clear that your audit should not be used as part of staff rationalisation or competency processes, or to make judgments on the effectiveness of individual TAs. This process is designed to illuminate the effects and consequences of your decision-making relating to matters of TAs' deployment, practice and preparation: the factors that enable or inhibit TAs in your schools from performing their role to maximum effect. Of course, if you are a headteacher new to post, these decisions will date back to your predecessor(s). These structures are inherited and may have evolved in a piecemeal fashion, rather than being decided strategically. Think of this decision-making layer as the lens through which you are gathering and analysing your data.

Conducting your audit

As a school leader, you will be alert to the sensitivities involved with auditing working practices. An underlying sense of judgment sometimes accompanies such an exercise, particularly one involving TAs, who are generally unaccustomed to the type of evaluative processes to which teachers are more readily accustomed. As we saw in Chapter 3, some TAs in some schools became anxious because it was unclear if and how their jobs would change as a result of MITA – and indeed, whether they would continue to have one.

We recommend undertaking your audit in a transparent way and that the messages about what is being scrutinised and evaluated, and the uses to which the audit findings will be put, are clear to your TAs. TAs' input is imperative, so it is important to apply gentle pressure to ensure they participate, while at the same time avoiding any heavy-handedness. Crucially, TAs need to feel that this is not something 'being done to them'. In particular, you should stress that it is *not* a staff rationalisation or competency process; it is emphatically not about making judgments on the effectiveness of individual TAs and their continued employment. TAs should be made aware they are contributing to and adding their voice to a valuable exercise to inform school improvement, and one that our work shows has considerable benefits for TAs.

Audit tools and process: *The TA Deployment Review Guide*

In previous versions of this book (e.g. Webster, Russell and Blatchford 2016), we set out a comprehensive audit process. In recent years, we have, on the basis of feedback from schools, refined this process and modified the audit tools. In this book, we provide a more streamlined process, which itself has been tested by hundreds of schools via the MITA programme. This process is captured in a document called the *TA Deployment Review Guide*, which is available to download from our website: www.maximisingtas.co.uk/resources.php.

We recommend that you follow the self-evaluation process specified in the *TA Deployment Review Guide*. We should state that in its entirety, this guidance lays out a six-step process for commissioning and a conducting a peer-to-peer TA deployment review. For the purposes of the process of an in-house self-evaluation, you need to focus only on steps 2 to 4.

To avoid any unnecessary duplication, we will not reproduce this guidance in this book, but we will summarise the review process and indicate how to use and access the audit tools.

Gathering your data

Self-evaluation

Complete the self-evaluation template in Annex 1 of the *TA Deployment Review Guide*. You might find it helpful to do this with at least one other member of your leadership team and/or your SENCO. The self-evaluation template is a thematic framework that invites you to benchmark your current practice against the best available research evidence. It asks you to identify areas of strength and areas for improvement. We encourage you to use the evaluation criteria as conversation starters; a starting point for reflecting on and talking about the nature and quality of TA deployment and practice, and the impact this has in your classrooms.

Hold in mind that your audit is a benchmark; a way to find your starting point. You are not identifying and promoting your achievements. Complete the self-evaluation honestly.

Staff survey

We strongly recommend that you administer our staff survey in order to obtain the experiences and views of teachers and TAs. In our experience, school leaders find this 'view from the shop floor' invaluable and informative. The survey questions, which have been developed and field-tested over several years by hundreds of schools, are designed to elicit typical patterns of deployment, opportunities for and levels of preparation (e.g. how confident TAs feel about their role), and perceptions of impact.

We advise that staff complete the survey anonymously in order to encourage openness and honesty. The survey asks TAs and teachers the same questions. The results will, therefore, show you how both groups experience deployment and preparation, and instantly show you where perceptions align and differ.

The surveys (one for TAs; one for teachers) can be found in Annex 2 of the *TA Deployment Review Guide*. More conveniently, there is an electronic version of the survey on our website, which you can set up and use within minutes. On the survey page, you will find a downloadable 'quick start guide' containing straightforward instructions on setting up and managing a survey.

To maximise your response rate, it could be worth setting aside some time in a staff meeting to allow staff to complete the survey at the same time. Alternatively, you could reserve a computer somewhere relatively private that TAs can use over the course of the week to complete the survey. Let them leave the classroom for ten minutes if they have to in order to get it done. Keep a list of names near the computer and ask TAs to tick their name off once they have done the survey. This is useful monitoring, while ensuring anonymity.

Observation

We understand that observing classroom practice is a sensitive area. However, in our experience and that of a number of schools that have thrived with MITA, the value of observation has helped enrich and deepen the picture provided by the results of the self-evaluation and staff survey. Relatedly, it was in the light of the findings from the DISS project lesson observations specifically that the research team were initially able to make sense of the troubling results on pupil progress.

Should you wish to conduct some form of observation, we would encourage you to focus some attention on the features of TAs' talk with pupils. We have produced a short observation tool, which is available on our website. It draws attention to the aspects of TAs' talk which are more and less effective, with the latter known to impede pupil learning and independence (e.g. spoon-feeding, and not providing adequate time to respond to a question).

Other evidence

We recommend that your audit includes the self-evaluation and staff survey, as a minimum. If conducting observations as suggested above might prove problematic, you could instead conduct some learning walks. Additionally, there are data from other sources that you could build into your audit; for example, book looks, or focus groups or interviews with small groups of TAs and teachers. This is a good way of exploring (sensitively) points of interest that arise from the results of your staff survey.

You should also scrutinise any relevant paperwork and policies, including TAs' job descriptions, role profiles and timetables. Other documents you might need to review include:

- Your school development plan
- Staffing structures and allocations (e.g. how TA capacity is distributed across year groups, subjects and classes)
- TA recruitment policy
- Terms and conditions of TA employment

- Induction and training processes for TAs, plus any staff training programmes
- Provision maps
- Your SEND information report and Pupil Premium statement.

Finally, some schools we have worked with have canvased pupils for their opinions or consulted them on proposed changes to TA deployment. Furthermore, you may wish to involve parents, particularly those of children with SEND, who are likely to be most affected by changes to the existing practice.

Monitoring and re-evaluation

In this short chapter we have provided you with the tools to conduct an audit of how TAs are presently deployed in your setting. Any process of change in any organisation needs to begin from a position of knowing what to change and the extent of change that will be needed. This will ensure resources are targeted effectively and the whole process is efficient.

Once you have set up your audit process, the tools can be used at routine intervals to monitor progress and to evaluate impact at one or more staging posts, essentially providing you with an 'after' picture to set alongside the 'before' picture.

Note

1 As you will have gathered, this book is not a school leadership manual, though it is informed by change management theories and processes. There are many books on school leadership available, but one we repeatedly turn to for inspiration is *Leadership Matters* by Andy Buck (2018).

Chapter 5

Supplementing, not replacing, the teacher

Deploying TAs differently

Introduction

Deployment concerns the decisions made about how TAs are used across the school and inside classrooms. The findings from the Deployment and Impact of Support Staff (DISS) project, which we summarised in Chapter 1, should leave us in no doubt that routine aspects of TA deployment need to be challenged and changed in order to avoid unintentionally damaging effects on pupils' academic progress. Decisions about TA deployment are the starting point from which all other decisions about TAs flow.

This is the premise of the key deployment question for school leaders, which we set out in Chapter 2, in terms of defining TAs' role, purpose and contribution. In this chapter, we provide some additional framing for this question and set out practical ideas to help explore it in depth. Our guidance and the exemplar strategies and approaches drawn from our MITA Journeys schools build on two key principles. Firstly, that TAs should not be used as an informal teaching resource for lower-attaining pupils and those with SEND. And secondly, that TAs should be deployed in ways that add value to what teachers do, not replace them. You will notice that these are the first two recommendations in the EEF guidance report we introduced in Chapter 1.

To reiterate, the findings from the DISS project led to stark conclusions about the role of TAs. It was clear that despite what we sometimes hear about teachers teaching and TAs supporting, TAs do have a direct, pedagogical role with pupils, which exceeds time spent supporting the teacher and curriculum, or performing other tasks. It is also clear that it is lower-attaining pupils (i.e. those not making expected levels of progress) and pupils identified as having SEND that TAs spent most time with.

This kind of individualised support from TAs might seem pedagogically valuable, but there are serious and unintended consequences, in terms of supported pupils having less time with, and receiving less input from, the teacher, and the knock-on impact this arrangement has on their academic progress, compared with typically-developing pupils. A term we often hear is that TA support is 'additional' to teacher input. The DISS project and subsequent research (Webster 2015; Blatchford and Webster 2018) has revealed, however, that TA support is *alternative* to teacher input.

In Chapter 2, we emphasised that the process of defining and delivering your vision must be driven by the strategic priorities relevant to *your* setting. Likewise, it will be shaped by factors that are unique to your context: your community; your cohorts; the individual needs of your pupils; and your staff. Given this, it is neither possible nor practical for us to provide a recipe for arriving at the perfect model of TA deployment.

What this chapter offers then is a set of layered processes and exemplars to provoke and inform your thinking and planning.

Considering the pedagogical role of TAs

As we discussed in Chapter 2, the process of reviewing and defining TAs' roles, while initiated and led by the SLT, must involve TAs and teachers. The audit process (Chapter 4) will help you to review the present deployment of TAs, and it will reveal the extent and form of TAs' present pedagogical role, and the contexts within which they teach. It will also identify any non-pedagogical roles they have, such as doing administrative tasks for teachers.

Given what we know from the DISS project, we might reasonably ask whether TAs should have a pedagogical role. Should they teach pupils directly? It is an important question, but in practical terms, we find it is somewhat redundant. Schools deploy TAs in a pedagogical capacity, and that seems unlikely to change. Tellingly though, our work with schools consistently reveals that TAs' pedagogical role can be more substantive than leaders imagine.

The question before us then is not whether TAs should have a pedagogical role, but what is the delineation of their pedagogical function? In other words, how can TAs add value to what happens in the classroom by supplementing rather than replacing teachers? In our view, this issue has been given too little attention, even though it is at the heart of many other issues connected to the employment and deployment of TAs. The second half of this chapter deals explicitly with the pedagogical role of TAs.

The pedagogical role TAs have with pupils must be precisely defined and agreed across the staff and governorship teams. Once it has, this position should be expressed formally as a policy. Your policy encapsulates and expands on your vision. Moreover, as with other school policies, it ensures consistency. In the absence of a vision or a policy, the situation on the ground risks variation – or confusion, as Knoster et al. (2000) put it (see Chapter 2) – across classes, with individual teachers making deployment decisions liable to contradict other decisions made by colleagues. We are, however, not suggesting that you implement a rigid policy that attempts to standardise all elements of practice across your school. What may be appropriate in a Year 6 class is unlikely to be workable in a Reception class. Accordingly, you ought to think in terms of broad principles that are operable across the school, and within which teachers in each class have freedom to develop practices that suit their respective context.

We discuss the TA deployment policy in detail shortly. Before we do, it is worth rehearsing the 'hard' questions that school leaders must address when using TAs in pedagogical contexts, which the research evidence compels us to not overlook.

Some important questions to ask about the pedagogical role of TAs

- Is it reasonable to expect TAs to be *as effective as* teachers when teaching pupils, given they do not have the same levels of training?
- Where is the appropriate boundary between the teaching roles of teachers and TAs?
- What is the limit, in terms of responsibility and accountability to parents and the school governing body, of TAs who teach?
- What does 'working under the supervision of the teacher' mean and look like in practice?

- Should teachers delegate the teaching of pupils with the most demanding learning needs to TAs, who generally do not possess the relevant professional qualifications?

Drawing up a policy on TA deployment

Your staff deserve clear and consistent guidance on TA deployment. We recommend you begin drafting your policy alongside the process set out in this book. You may already have some ideas worth capturing, and these will be shaped and clarified by the discussions you have with staff and governors, and the things you pilot in classrooms. The process of the policy's development and its implementation creates a shared understanding of the boundaries between the roles of teachers and TAs, in terms of how the TAs can expect to be managed by teachers to maximum benefit. Be mindful of taking an over-prescriptive approach. Some level of autonomy and flexibility will be necessary. Think, where possible, in terms of a framework within which staff can operate.

MITA Journeys

A flexible framework

After a year of preparation and small-scale trialling, Laureate moved away from the one class, one TA model to a phase base approach, with TA deployment driven instead by pupil need. TA deployment was rethought through a lens of fairness for pupils. As Dave Perkins, the Head-teacher, explained:

> The fairness has got to be what's fair for the pupils; to get the support that they need in order to achieve the outcomes that we want them to be able to achieve.

As teachers did not have a TA with them all the time, deployment needed to be more fluid, with freer movement of TAs across classes and lessons. For instance, the teachers and the Key Stage leader look at assessment data in order to plan and direct the three TAs in the Key Stage 1 and 2 team. Dave reported:

> We are not proscriptive about timetabling TAs, but for argument's sake, we might have one TA doing a carpet input for ten minutes, then popping next door and do eight minutes with that teacher, then come back in to help with the independent learning.

He added that the worries some teachers had, about whether this flexibility would negatively impact the TAs' knowledge of pupils, have not materialised:

> A genuine concern was whether TAs are going to know the children as well to be able to interact with them if they're not in the class the whole time, but that hasn't been a problem at all.

At Shirley Manor, the allocation of TAs to classes was similarly determined on a case-by-case basis. As Headteacher, Heather Lacey, explained:

We don't have a teaching assistant per classroom. The TA is there for need, so it depends on the need of the classroom. I've got some classes with three TAs; I've got two that share a part-time TA. It goes on what that cohort needs, at that particular time.

The approaches at Laureate and Shirley Manor not only shifted the conversation away from teacher need ('the TA as PA' [personal assistant] model, as Dave put it) to pupil need, but also put greater emphasis on teams and trust. As Heather explained, each class team "knows *what* they're doing, *when* they're doing it, *who* they should be doing it with."

You may decide that rather than write a separate policy, you will expand and integrate the necessary content relating to TAs into existing policies, such as your teaching and learning policy, or your marking and feedback policy. Either way, as it is helpful to have some sense of what that content might look like, we have prepared an editable TA policy template that you can download from our website. It specifies the areas we think a comprehensive TA deployment policy ought to cover and some suggestions to consider.

Your policy should be a 'living' document, embodying what you do in relation to the employment and deployment of your TA workforce. It does not need to run to pages and pages. In fact, as a number of schools we have worked with have discovered, concision is key. You could, for example, distil your policy into a one-page summary, setting out what TAs can expect from SLT, what TAs can expect from teachers, and what the SLT and teachers can expect from TAs. An example document can be found in Appendix 1 and also on our website. Whichever approach you take, avoid the temptation to 'cut and paste'. As we said in Chapter 2, the needs and strategic priorities of your setting are different to those of other settings. Your policy must reflect *your* vision for *your* school throughout.

You will, of course, need to communicate your policy. We addressed the key considerations regarding this earlier in the book, stressing the importance of thorough and open processes of consultation, information gathering, decision making, discussion and implementation involving staff. Pupils will also need to be made aware of the ways in which your school will deploy TAs, since some may have become dependent on them. Where models of TA deployment depart from previous practice, teachers will need to explain new forms of teamwork to their class. Parents should also be included in this process, particularly those of children with an EHCP who may have become familiar with – or expect – particular models of TA deployment and support. Where families feel they have had to fight long and hard to obtain individual TA support for their child, they are likely to be concerned, anxious, perhaps even defensive, if they perceive that this is at risk. The benefits of new or modified approaches (e.g. that it will lead to more time with the teacher) will need to be clearly justified and explained. You might find the support of an educational psychologist helpful in mediating this (see Webster 2014).

Key recommendations on developing a policy on TA deployment

- With your SLT, address the hard questions listed above and use the answers to frame your philosophy on TA deployment.

- Draft a policy on TA deployment, setting out a framework within which teachers will have some flexibility at the classroom level. Be clear about how class teachers will be able to deploy TAs and what is no longer permissible.
- Modify your draft policy as you work through the MITA process to reflect what you learn about what works and what does not work.

Clarifying the role of each TA

Decisions about staffing structure

Many schools have cited the need to overhaul their staffing structure as a reason for participating in our MITA programme. We often work with incoming headteachers who are new to post and who have inherited a workforce containing a high number of TAs, mainly on part-time contracts. Commonly, this situation is a legacy of a long-serving predecessor. As the evidence on TA deployment and impact matures, we find that school leaders are increasingly being moved to take more deliberate and conscious decisions regarding the deployment of TAs, moving away from the routine default position of deploying all TAs on the same basis in a generic role, to a more purposeful and methodical alignment of specific roles and individuals.

It is essential you base any decisions about the staffing structure in your setting on a careful analysis of the needs of all your pupils. When it comes to ensuring the best learning outcomes for the most vulnerable pupils, your first line of defence is high-quality teaching, planned for and delivered by your teachers. The MITA journey, perhaps paradoxically, starts not with TAs at all, but with teachers and how they meet the needs of pupils.

Defining the needs of the pupils in your school

The needs of your pupils are many and varied, but you and your SLT will be able to make a broad list of needs that might include, but not be limited to, the ways all pupils need to acquire:

- a secure foundation in reading, writing, spelling, language and numeracy
- knowledge and competence across a broad range of curriculum subjects
- attentiveness and listening skills
- an enquiring mind
- a sense of entitlement to, and appetite for, knowledge and self-improvement
- metacognitive skills (i.e. knowing how to know, or learning how to learn)
- information handling skills (e.g. how to evaluate evidence and its sources)
- confidence in the face of challenges
- mental toughness to cope with uncertainty
- strength to accept failure as part of learning
- independent working skills and self-reliance
- an understanding and acceptance of boundaries
- skills to interact and collaborate with others
- skills to maintain positive relationship with peers
- skills for honest self-reflection.

There will be a smaller group of pupils, principally those with SEND, who have specific needs that must be met, but which are not directly related to learning. These needs might include, but not be limited to: physical and/or sensory impairments; mental health; well-being and emotional needs; and difficulties with speech and language. Ensure you list these needs too.

Determining roles and responsibilities

Here is an exercise you can do as an SLT. Draw a Venn diagram on a large sheet of paper or on a whiteboard. Label one circle *'Teachers' role and responsibilities'*, and label the other circle *'TAs' role and contribution'*. At this point, avoid using the word 'responsibility' in relation to TAs, as the language of accountability is not helpful here. Now map the items on your list of pupils' needs that are clearly within the teachers' sphere of responsibility onto the teacher circle of your diagram. Debate the items on the list that are left over and place them on the diagram. Can you agree and clarify a boundary around the teachers' role and responsibilities? What space opens up around the TAs' role, and what sort of contribution might they be able to make to meet the needs of pupils? Look for ways in which TAs can 'add value' to what teachers do.

Oftentimes there will be roles that fall in the intersect. This is indicative of the reality in schools; things do not drop neatly into boxes labelled 'things only teachers do' and 'things only TAs do'. You may need to interrogate some of these activities further and break them down into subprocesses, before deciding how these are defined and distributed, on the basis of where the balance of accountability lies. For example, acquiring reading skills requires: direct instruction of skills (phonics and comprehension); planning for groups and individuals; listening to individual readers; monitoring and recording progress; assessing progress; planning intervention programmes; and delivering intervention programmes. These are roles that TAs and teachers often divide between them. The key is to ensure that the TA's share of the overall role (e.g. acquiring reading skills) does not lead to them absorbing a disproportionate amount of responsibility for the outcomes.

You can do the Venn exercise with your teachers and TAs, either separately or together. One approach is to ask your teaching staff to envisage the classroom as it would be *without* a TA. How would they organise things in order to provide the best educational experience for *all* pupils in the class, including those typically supported by a TA? Next, figuratively speaking, reintroduce the TA to the classroom. What can they do to help teaching and learning, and/or to help keep the classroom running efficiently and effectively *without* replacing the teacher?

MITA Journeys

Venn diagram exercise

The staff at Crestwood undertook the Venn diagram exercise, using hula hoops to create two overlapping circles. The SLT used the diagram that the staff created as the basis for the school's policy on TA deployment. Both the diagram and the process of creating it highlighted how the combined efforts of TAs and teachers and working together were essential for giving their pupils the best chance of reaching and exceeding their potential. The policy recognised the value each member of the team brings in terms of their knowledge, expertise and experience. The teachers reported that this early part of the MITA process helped to reinforce a 'team mentality'.

This exercise helps schools to think through the fundamentals of the TA role, purpose and contribution from the perspective of pupil need. This change of emphasis matters because schools can understandably get stuck on the idea of finding and justifying roles for every TA. But this positions adults as the focus of decision-making, rather than the pupils. As uncomfortable as this can be to confront, it is important to acknowledge that the process of rethinking your staffing structure *on the basis of a clear analysis of pupils' needs* – as opposed to the needs of TAs themselves – *could* result in some TAs having their hours of work reduced or some roles becoming surplus to requirement. That said, in practice, we rarely see this happen. Overall TA capacity is more likely to be redistributed than reduced.

Such planning should, as best as possible, take account of future needs and future cohorts. You will need to consider how your most heavily supported pupils (i.e. those with an EHCP) will develop in years to come; how their needs may change, and what (and how much) support you anticipate might be needed. Also, national and local pupil projection data can predict population bulges and which types of SEND may be on the increase or decline.

Of course, there is a place for considering the needs of adults too – specifically your teachers. TAs will be needed to ensure your teachers are freed up to deliver high-quality teaching, for instance. Below we address specific points to consider how TAs can be deployed in direct and indirect ways (i.e. pedagogical and non-pedagogical roles) to ensure the needs of pupils are met. But first, we set out the two main ways in which you and your SLT can approach decisions about determining your staffing structure.

The 'blank page' approach

What we have termed the 'blank page' approach assumes you are starting from scratch, as if you were setting up a brand new school. With freedom to determine everything about the composition and nature of your yet-to-be-appointed TA workforce, you can decide the staffing structure you require in order to meet your pupils' needs. Questions you need to ask include:

- How many TAs do you want to have a predominantly pedagogical role, and how will they be assigned (e.g. to classes, subjects and/or year groups; to the delivery of interventions)?
- Do you require TAs to provide short-term lesson cover for teachers? If so, how many TAs are needed for this?
- How many TAs are needed to support pupils with physical/mobility and/or sensory needs?
- How many TAs do you require to have an ostensibly non-pedagogical role to assist with things like cookery, art and school trips, and/or in a welfare or pastoral role (e.g. for a nurture group)?

Some schools we know have found it helpful to use the Professional Standards for Teaching Assistants[1] and TA role profiles provided by their local authority, which outline the key 'responsibilities' and entry-level requirements for TAs at several graded levels, to help make decisions about staffing. Using the blank page approach, you will be able to establish a broad set of essential TA roles, which are distinct from one another and from the role of teachers. Much will depend on the number of pupils you have on roll and the range of need, but a good rule of thumb is to limit the overall number of role types to around four. We consider role types for TAs below, but it is worth mentioning here that it is an approach a small number of schools like to adopt. One school, for instance, shaped job descriptions around three categories: general class-based, specialists for complex SEND and interventions, and nurture. The roles had a common core, but diverged in relation to their substantive and specific purpose.

The next step is to map your existing TAs on to the roles you identified in the exercise above, using the evidence from your audit of TAs' skills and qualifications. Some TAs have strengths in providing warmth, empathy and encouragement, and have a firm but sensitive authority, which would make them suited to working with pupils in nurturing roles. Other TAs may have a degree in a particular subject specialism and would be suitably deployed to support lessons in that subject.

The key principle is to develop roles more consciously and purposefully, and to ensure and specify the minimum level of expertise expected for each role. Every effort must be made to avoid defaulting to the current and widespread – not to mention ineffective – forms of TA deployment, which do not vary across year groups, classes, subjects or the individuals who occupy these roles.

There may be roles that are not filled by individuals, and, conversely, TAs who do not have roles within your new structure. However, this process will highlight training needs for specific individuals, who can be skilled up to meet the role requirements.

The 'retrofit' approach

We call the second approach to deciding your staffing structure the 'retrofit' approach. This process is essentially the reverse of the 'blank page' approach, as you begin by building your staffing structure on the basis of the skills of your existing TA workforce. It is important to note this approach will not necessarily give your school the TA staffing structure you *need* or one that aligns with any idealised model; in other words, it is somewhat less consistent with centring your approach on putting the needs of pupils first. However, it does allow you to start from existing strengths and to identify gaps, which can then be planned for.

While the starting point for the retrofit approach is to confirm the levels at which your TAs are working, we find that some schools use TA role profiles to initiate this exercise: to ascertain whether TAs are being deployed in line with or are stretched (perhaps unfairly or unreasonably) beyond their current capabilities, as well as to identify any training gaps.

Consultation

Changing your TA staffing structure may involve wider consultations as inevitable modifications to contracts and conditions of employment have legal ramifications. Some local authorities have a policy and/or adviser on staff restructure who leaders of maintained schools could refer to. Academies and other schools who cannot access such local authority services may have to consult their own advisers on employment law. It may also be necessary to consult with local union representatives (e.g. Unison).

At the school level, school leaders may not be able to implement changes without approval from the governing body or board of trustees. Governors and trustees are often consulted on developments that have financial implications. On this issue, we note that restructuring your TA workforce may incur some short-term costs (which would be offset by long-term gains), but we know of no legal bar to this.

Key recommendations on clarifying the role of each TA

- Conduct a survey of TAs' skills, qualifications and training received as part of your audit.
- Review the current TA roles and consider having a select number of distinct role types within a new staffing structure.
- Conduct appropriate consultations with legal and union representatives, and the school's governing body or board of trustees.

Role types for TAs

In this section, we discuss the main types of role in which TAs are most effectively deployed. We consider roles that are broadly pedagogical and non-pedagogical in nature, and which can have, respectively, direct and indirect impact on pupil outcomes. We illustrate how schools have operationalised these roles and reveal the thinking that went into these decisions, beginning with non-pedagogical roles.

Non-pedagogical roles

The research evidence suggests three main non-pedagogical roles TAs can adopt (see Blatchford, Russell and Webster 2012):

1   Supporting teachers by carrying out routine tasks, such as preparing and organising materials
2   Helping with classroom organisation and ensuring lessons run smoothly by encouraging pupils to focus on tasks and 'nipping in the bud' any off-task or disruptive behaviour
3   Supporting pupils with physical/mobility, sensory, and/or emotional needs.

As we indicated earlier in this chapter, the established trend in the UK (and elsewhere) is for schools to deploy TAs in pedagogical roles. While the virtual caricature of the TA whose duties centred on washing out paint-pots, doing first aid, and helping out in the library is a relic of the late-twentieth century, there are justifiable reasons why some schools may consider a mainly non-pedagogical role for a small number of their TAs. Let us look at each of these four types of role in turn.

Supporting teachers with administrative support

Perhaps the most extreme expression of a non-pedagogical role is one that requires little, if any, interaction with pupils, and instead is aimed at helping teachers with their routine clerical tasks (photocopying, etc.). We know from the DISS project that such deployment of TAs and other support staff contributed to reducing teacher workloads and positively affected their levels of stress and job satisfaction (Blatchford, Russell and

Webster 2012). When TAs take on teachers' routine admin tasks, it frees up time for teachers to focus on teaching tasks, such as lesson planning and assessment. This, in turn, improves their teaching. We refer to this form of TA support as having an *indirect* impact on pupils: TAs help teachers to help pupils.

No school leader would deploy their entire current TA workforce in this way, but there may be a case for developing, say, one TA post for this type of work. Given the attention on teacher workload and wellbeing, it is worth holding in mind whether your teachers could benefit from one of your TAs being deployed, even part-time, to ease their admin burden. It could even be an attractive feature of your teacher recruitment and/or retention strategy.

Supporting teachers with classroom management

Another way in which TAs in a non-pedagogical role can benefit teachers is evident in the findings from the DISS project on classroom management. We have known for some time that the main behaviour problem in schools is the 'persistent, low level disruption of lessons that wears down staff and disrupts learning' (Ofsted 2005; 2014). Encouragingly, the DISS project found that the presence of a TA limited the need for teachers to manage this kind of problem. Low level disruption can be greatly reduced when TAs are deployed to manage off-task behaviour and ensure pupils are focused, attentive and on-task. This gives teachers more time to teach, thus benefiting everyone in the class. In our experience, this is more of an issue in secondary schools than primary schools, nevertheless, there may be a case for developing an effective non-pedagogical role for TAs along these lines: TAs acting as an extra set of eyes and ears, noticing unwanted behaviour, and stepping in to address it without disrupting the teacher's delivery or the flow of the lesson.

We note, however, that while Giangreco and Broer (2005) found in their research that TAs spent one-fifth of their time providing behavioural support to pupils, they were relatively untrained and underprepared in this area; they often lacked confidence when it came to managing challenging behaviour, too. If you develop such a role for all or some of your TAs, it is imperative they are thoroughly trained in classroom management techniques and are recognised by staff and pupils as legitimate enforcers of the school's expectations regarding behaviour. Teachers, of course, must retain the ultimate responsibility for motivating pupils, gaining and maintaining their focus, and be responsible for behaviour management overall (and especially for serious incidents); it is not a duty to be wholly delegated to TAs. However, there are ways in which the TA can watch for those small signs of negative and off-task behaviour, and step in to address it without disrupting the lesson.

This form of TA deployment will need to be responsive to the emerging needs of the pupils across any particular lesson, and be sensitive to how your teachers prefer to deal with behaviour. Teachers should agree the appropriate forms of intercession with the TA (s) in their class. In the most effective instances we have seen, TAs are able to discreetly capture the attention of disruptive or off-task pupils, and with a look, a gesture or a whisper, quell the disquiet. We have seen many examples of TAs dampen potentially volatile situations, refocus off-task pupils, break up chatter, confiscate sweets, and move pupils to other seats. This limits the distracting effects of individual pupils, and generally keeps the classroom ticking over, allowing the teacher to teach and pupils to learn.

Teachers should include the TA in the sanctions and rewards policy they use for their class (which should, of course, be in line with whole-school strategies), but ensure there is consistency; pupils are quick to pick up on variations in consequences for the same misdemeanour. Either way, teachers must demonstrate that they and the TA are a team and that teachers back TAs' judgments. It will need to be clear to pupils that TAs have the power to deal with low-level disruption and that they are to be respected and obeyed in this capacity. In the worst cases we have seen and had described to us, pupils undermine both the teacher, and particularly the TA, when they play the teacher's seniority off against the TA's relatively weaker position.

The appropriate use of TAs as classroom behaviour monitors should be explicitly covered in your relevant policies. The limits of the role must be made clear; for example, you might specify that TAs may move a pupil to another desk, but decisions to send them from the classroom must only be taken by teachers. This, together with coaching and mentoring support from teachers, and underpinned by a consistent approach to consequences and rewards, is what really gives TAs confidence.

You should also consider the extent to which TAs supporting classroom management should engage in pedagogical support. To what extent should they help pupils who are stuck, or need help with the task they are attempting? Teachers and TAs should develop a clear understanding of what types of pedagogical support the TA should provide, and when they should encourage the pupil to ask for teacher support instead. For example, TAs could help where a pupil needs support with working out what to do next, but if they need a concept re-explained, they should ask the teacher.

Supporting pupils' physical, sensory and/or emotional needs

Some TAs in some schools will already have a role related to the support of pupils with physical or sensory needs (e.g. mobility, visual or hearing impairment). We also consider such support to have an *indirect* impact on learning, as it helps the supported pupil to access teaching and learning in a physical and/or dispositional sense.

TAs working in this role require, and will likely have received, special training in, for example: handling; physiotherapy techniques; sign language; or using special equipment. Such support from TAs is vital for these pupils who attend mainstream settings; not due to a learning need, but because of accessibility issues relating to the buildings, equipment and aspects of the curriculum.

The issue for school leaders to consider is this: what proportion of the time do TAs in such roles *actually* spend supporting pupils' physical and/or sensory needs, and what proportion of the time do they do other things? While there is clear value in TAs performing roles many teachers will not be able to do concurrent with leading the class (e.g. signing for hearing impaired pupils), the research evidence suggests that where teachers leave TAs to, for example, unfold a mobility chair or set up radio aids, their responsibilities, over time, extend to pedagogical functions for which they are less prepared.

While we do not understate the need for necessary forms of physical and sensory support, our research has raised concerns about the assumptions teachers of mainstream classes make about the need for, and level of, support they should provide for pupils with such needs. Although it is true not all pupils with physical and sensory needs have learning needs, many do. And although TAs who support such pupils have often had specialist training to assist such needs, it should not be assumed they have had quality training to support pupils' learning needs as well (Anderson and Finney 2008; Lamb 2009; Norwich and Lewis 2001). Michael Giangreco (2003) refers to this as the 'training trap': the tendency for teachers to relinquish instruction of pupils with SEND to TAs who have received more or less any kind of training, no matter how scant. We do not pretend that getting the right balance is straightforward, but if a TA has been appointed to provide, for example, physical support, it needs to be clear that the teacher is predominantly responsible for the pedagogical support.

This speaks to issues concerning the preparedness of TAs, which we shall address in Chapter 7. However, the point to make here in relation to deployment is that when teachers fall into the training trap, it increases the separation between teachers and TA-supported pupils, the unintended and troubling effects we described in Chapter 1.

Your audit will reveal whether there is capacity for TAs in such roles to perform other roles at times when they are not supporting pupils' physical needs. For example, if the supported pupil is able to work independently in a lesson, this creates an opportunity for the TA to assist the teacher or other pupils in another way. Again, it is important that if you decide to expand the role of these TAs, it must be clear to them and teachers what the extended limits of their new role are, and these new responsibilities must be supported by training.

TAs that support pupils' emotional needs must have well delineated roles. We know of schools that deploy TAs in nurturing roles in order to bridge gaps between a pupil's emergent and challenging needs and the demands of the classroom. TAs in these 'key worker' or 'link worker' roles provide a stable and containing presence to help children self-regulate; some may deliver specific programmes aimed at exploring and developing pupils' emotional literacy and coping skills. Given the increase in the proportion of pupils experiencing some form of social, emotional or mental health need in our schools, we think this particular expression of the paraprofessional role has potential. That said, the supplement/replace issue is as salient here as it is in the context of instructional support. TAs should not be deployed in place of professionals, such as counsellors, to deal with pupils' complex emotional problems. That said, we see no reason why, with proper training and support, TAs cannot provide invaluable supplementary support to these wider processes, helping pupils to share thoughts and feelings on a day-to-day basis.

Results from the DISS project showed teachers value the knowledge TAs have of pupils, because they work so closely with them and therefore hear about important things in their life that influence their mood and wellbeing. Additionally, TAs often have knowledge about pupils based on the fact that they live in the same neighbourhood; unlike teachers, who are more likely to live out of the school's catchment area. Therefore, TAs can be more aware of how family and community life affect pupils.

Fraser and Meadows (2008) found pupils characterised the best TAs as demonstrating care, kindliness, friendliness, helpfulness, warmth and attentiveness. Dunne et al. (2008) highlight TAs' functional priorities in terms of a predominantly nurturing role. Therefore, it is perhaps unsurprising that we have found interactions between TAs and pupils are often less formal and more intimate than those between teachers and pupils; pupils viewed TAs as being closer to 'their level' than teachers.

Many TAs have the background and dispositions well suited to supporting pupils' pastoral needs, and you may choose to develop some specific non-pedagogical roles to capitalise on this. We are aware of a number of schools that train TAs to become Emotional Literacy Support Assistants (ELSAs). TAs qualify following a structured programme of training and supervision from educational psychologists. ELSAs plan and deliver individual and small group support programmes to help pupils with social and emotional difficulties to recognise, understand and manage their emotions, to increase their wellbeing and success in school. While such roles are underpinned by training and support, we argue there are particular risks that can stem from TAs selecting, planning, delivering and assessing interventions with little input from teachers, of which you need to be aware. We address TA-led interventions in Chapter 8.

Parent support

Parental support and engagement are critical factors in how well children achieve. Schools have long been concerned with the lack of engagement exhibited by some parents in their child's learning. In some cases, this can be explained by parents' own negative experiences of school and learning. As we have mentioned, a school typically draws its TA workforce from the catchment area it serves. This, together with the personal qualities listed above, puts TAs in a strong position to act as effective mediators or 'connectors' between the school and parents.

One school we worked with had a sizable cohort of pupils whose attendance was quite poor. The headteacher was spending a considerable amount of her time unsuccessfully chasing up absences each morning. One of the TAs, who had worked at the school for over 30 years (and had even been a pupil there herself), knew the local community and its history well. She was a trusted figure and well-liked by the parents of the pupils with concerningly low rates of attendance. She was ideally suited to take on a newly-created attendance monitoring role. She would call parents, and (if needed) drive to houses and get children out of bed and into school. This process not only freed up valuable headteacher time, but it was markedly more successful, as the TA was better able to negotiate the cultural barriers.

It is beyond the scope of this book to provide guidance on developing a parent support role for TAs. Our intention is only to raise the possibility that there might be capacity within your TA workforce to create such a role(s), if the needs of your school community require it. If this is of interest, you might like to consider a home–liaison role along the lines of a local authority portage scheme, or a role in family interventions, such as the Positive Parenting Programme.

Key recommendations on defining non–pedagogical roles for TAs

- Define the remit of non-pedagogical roles; for example, in terms of the routine tasks TAs should and should not do; or the appropriate level of intervention in managing behaviour.
- When thinking about how TAs can add value to teaching, capitalise on things TAs are well placed to do (e.g. monitor behaviour while the teacher is teaching).
- Look for efficiencies in TA time. Are there other things they could be doing when they are not, for example, supporting a pupil's physical needs?
- Ensure pupils are clear about the role of the TA, and that teachers and TAs adopt a team approach.
- Ensure any role change or extension is supported by training and is consistent with school policies (e.g. on behaviour management).

Defining a pedagogical role for TAs

It is an established fact that the vast majority of TAs in our schools have been recruited to and are deployed in pedagogical contexts. As we raised earlier with our 'hard' questions on deploying TAs in pedagogical roles, this prompts a set of pedagogical, practical, philosophical and ethical issues that school leaders need to address in relation to the composition and parameters of TAs' pedagogical role. We summarise these below before exploring each in turn:

- What role should TAs have as part of the school's provision for lower-attaining pupils and those with SEND?
- What is the role of TAs (and teachers) in planning, delivering and assessing intervention programmes?
- Do we want TAs to lead classes as part of the school's PPA and/or short-term teacher cover arrangements?
- Should we change the allocation of TAs across classes, year groups and/or subjects, and how do we make best use of TAs in these contexts?
- Are changes needed to TAs' job specifications, conditions of employment and salaries? How will these changes affect TAs already in post and any future appointments?

You may decide that some individual TAs should have different pedagogical responsibilities, based on their respective skills of working with whole classes, groups and individuals. These skills sets may vary across your TA workforce. For example, given the results of your audit of TAs' skills, some might be more appropriately deployed to lead classes as part of PPA arrangements than others. In which case, you will need to ask the questions above with individual TAs in mind in order to determine the limitations of their pedagogical role. TAs may have particular strengths in specific curriculum areas, but do not assume being qualified to degree level in a particular subject means someone is able to teach or advance learning. This is another expression of the 'training trap'.

The questions above are useful for determining the outermost limits of the pedagogical role; in other words: given the need to maintain a distinction between the two, just how far should the TAs' teaching role extend into the territory of the teachers' teaching role? Many teachers have a view about the encroachment of TAs on their professional teaching role – some are more positive than others (see Blatchford, Russell and Webster 2012) – but rarely do they look this issue full in the face and make decisions about how it affects their classroom practice. It is important, therefore, to set a school-level context or framework for teacher decisions at the classroom level (we have mentioned already the need for autonomy and flexibility), and in no case is this more important than when considering the provision of pupils with SEND.

Pupils with SEND

If the pedagogical function is one established fact about the role of TAs, then another fact that is beyond doubt is that they are critical to the way schools meet the educational needs of pupils with SEND. Often deployed *in place of* teachers, evidence relating to pupils with the highest level of need (i.e. those with an EHCP) shows that TAs, in effect, take on the role of primary educator. This in turn produces a marginalising effect in terms of time with TAs cutting across – or replacing – time in class, with the teacher, in main curriculum coverage, and with peers (Webster 2015; Blatchford and Webster 2018).

Teachers must become the adult with whom pupils with SEND have regular interaction, and these pupils must remain part of the teaching and learning experience provided in the classroom as much as possible. As a school leader, and in line with the SEND Code of Practice (DfE/DoH 2015), it is your responsibility to uphold this requirement. While SENCOs should be teachers' first port of call for help and support, it is not for them (or TAs for that matter) to do their job for them. You should make it clear you will be looking for evidence of teachers taking responsibility for the teaching and learning of *all* pupils as part of your monitoring processes.

In the section that follows, we describe some relatively simple changes to deployment routines to reduce the instances and effects of separation for pupils with SEND. It is worth restating that, while these models of classroom organisation were developed principally with these pupils in mind, they are transferrable and applicable to any and all pupil groups.

MITA Journeys

Undoing the Velcro

The MITA Journeys schools all took seriously the issue of the 'Velcro effect'. As Amy Cooper, former Deputy, now Headteacher at Crestwood, explained:

> At first, some of the TAs were a little bit concerned, because they thought if they weren't sitting next to someone and doing something all the time, people might think that they weren't doing anything.

So entrenched and automatic were some practices, that it took time, encouragement and support to get TAs to a position where they not only knew when to withdraw and allow space for pupils to work independently, but were comfortable with doing so. A TA at Shirley Manor conjured an image of support being 'like an elastic band': 'pulling away a little bit, but they come back a little bit'.

As Dave Perkins at Laureate said, 'it takes a conscious effort', and not just from the TAs, but from the teachers too, who must be mindful that 'those more vulnerable children are getting more teacher time'. He explained that the move away from high intensity, one-to-one support for pupils with an EHCP was 'a selling point' to parents: 'If they're not Velcroed to the TA, they're having more teacher time.' Referring to a pupil with an EHCP who had recently joined Year 3, Dave explained:

> We were very clear with the parents that unless there is a specific safety or medical dis- ability need, we don't do one-to-ones, because we want him to be as independent as possible. We explained that there will be adults there to support him; sometimes that might be the teacher and sometimes that might be the TA.

Interestingly, the school also talked with the external professionals involved with pupils with EHCPs, so that they could encourage this model of support:

> For a child who is hearing impaired, the professional will come along [to an annual review] and be advocating for mum that this is what your child is entitled to, and trying to help them understand that we try to build pupil independence. We would never not support them, but actually this model of growing their independence is more supportive, because it's more sustainable for them as a learner and as a young person.

Deploying TAs differently

In the section, we unpack some alternative ways of deploying TAs in classrooms, and provide further examples and experiences of the TAs, teachers and leaders of MITA Journeys schools. Consistent with our overarching philosophy of deploying TAs in ways that supplement rather than replace teachers, the approaches and ideas below are based on the principles of: (i) working towards to a situation where the pupils with the greatest level of need have *at least* the same amount of time with teachers as their peers; and (ii) ensuring the lower-attaining pupils and those with SEND are not routinely and unnecessarily separated from the teacher and the classroom.

Withdrawal from the class

Firstly, we draw attention to a common arrangement we have witnessed in many schools, and which ought to be avoided wherever possible: the routine removal of pupils – typically those with SEND and low attainers – from the classrooms to work with the TA. On occasion, there is good reason for taking pupils out of the classroom to work in a nearby shared area or corridor, say; for example, where an activity requires more space than there is in the room. What the evidence has prompted for us is a concern about the routineness of withdrawal; the way it gets habituated and used as a classroom management strategy – even when there is no call for it.

TAs are frequently deployed as an informal teaching resource for individual pupils and small groups. Teachers need to reverse this situation: *they* must become the adult with whom pupils with SEND have regular, sustained and focused interactions. Rather than routinely assigning the TA to teach the pupils with the greatest learning needs – and thus require professional input – teachers will have to ensure the TA works with pupils across the class as a whole. This allows the teacher the opportunity to interact regularly with these pupils for prolonged periods. We know from our work with schools that teachers can greatly improve and enrich their understanding of the learning needs and progress of pupils who previously worked more often with the TA than the teacher (Webster, Blatchford and Russell 2013).

Rotating across the week

Teachers can address the tendency for TAs to routinely support lower attaining groups and pupils with SEND by widening the range of contexts in which they are deployed.; specifically, using TAs to support groups of higher attaining, average attaining and mixed attaining groups. One effective strategy we have seen in primary classrooms involves the teachers deploying themselves and the TA on a rotational basis. Here, both adults work with a different group each day throughout the week. The teacher could set independent and group work tasks for the tables without an adult present, and over the course of the week, each group has roughly the same amount of time being supported by the teacher, supported by the TA, working with peers and working independently.

MITA Journeys

Introducing mixed attainment grouping

In three of our five MITA Journey schools, the MITA process was accompanied by a move away from grouping pupils on the basis of ability to mixed attainment grouping. TAs were attuned to the problems of within-class ability grouping, as one TA from Laureate described:

> We'd always seen that as a bit of an issue... If you're grouping those children together, who are they learning off?... If you're putting the same ability children together – and starting from Key Stage 1 – you're automatically picking their social groups as well... And it gives them a label, doesn't it? They know they're in the low ability group, and they know they're sat on that table.

Coupled with the practice of not routinely withdrawing pupils with SEND and low attainers, moving to mixed attainment teaching marked a shift to a more inclusive teaching and learning experience. TAs in these schools noted that not being routinely deployed to work with the 'bottom' group gave them opportunities to work with pupils across the attainment range. They got to know each child and their needs. Plus, as one TA at Cuddington Croft observed, 'it's great because for the child, or the children, as they get to know their peers a lot more, and I think that's invaluable.'

A teacher at Cuddington Croft explained that the TAs working in Years 5 and 6 initially 'doubted their subject knowledge' and feared they might struggle with supporting groups of mixed attaining pupils:

> But actually, once we got into it, the TAs responded really well... It meant for us, we were able to spend more time with the children that needed us the most, because the TA was making sure the other children were on track, or were being challenged.

Leaders, TAs and teachers all commented on the way the pupils' perception of TAs changed. As one teacher at Shirley Manor said: 'The children now see them as an extra adult to help them, rather than just one child.'

Teaching triage

During classwork, TAs tend to remain in one place working with a group or individual, while the teacher moves about the classroom, ensuring pupils are on-task and progressing. Here is a variation on this approach that sees these roles flipped, and the TA deployed in a 'triaging' capacity. The TA can bring to the teacher's attention particular individuals who are having difficulty with the task while the teacher spends extended time with another group. Once alerted, the teacher can move in to provide targeted support while the TA continues to rove the room.

MITA Journeys

Live marking

When roving the classroom, TAs at Cuddington Croft were deployed to contribute to live marking in lessons. As one teacher described, this encouraged 'a dialogue with the TA at the point of teaching.' As well as being able to cover all children and all groups between them, the instant nature of the feedback meant that it was more impactful. Scott Maclean, the Head-teacher, reported that the school had 'talked a lot about marking and feedback' with teachers in relation to MITA, drawing attention to the workload benefits, too:

> If you can skill up your TA and work in partnership with them, they can do some of that marking and feedback for you in the lesson. Therefore, you've got maybe six fewer books to mark at the end. Actually, that's freeing up your time... Marking's reduced for the teachers, because they're not having to take 90 books home with them anymore.

TAs leading classes

One of the more contentious issues arising out of the 2003 National Agreement to address teacher workload was the idea that TAs could lead classes as part of arrangements to facilitate PPA time or to cover short-term absences. In a very visible way, TAs were seen to replace teachers, even though the nature of the work – labelled 'supervision' – was described in such a way as to make it distinct from 'teaching'. However, it was clear that when TAs led classes, they took on a teaching role, much as they did when they were working with individuals or groups (Blatchford, Russell and Webster 2012). In many cases, this was inevitable; pupils keen to get on with the work left for them by the teacher, asked TAs for explanations or clarifications of concepts relating to the task.

Leading classes gives the TA a role that clearly overlaps with that of the teacher, in terms of having class-level responsibility and interactions. The aim of the restructuring process described in this book is to create roles for TAs that are distinct from, but complementary to, the teachers' role and responsibilities. Our position on this is that deploying TAs to cover lessons should be done as a last resort; the first response should be to ensure a qualified teacher leads learning. That said, we are fully aware that there are an increasing set of circumstances linked to dwindling school budgets that make this exceptionally difficult. Therefore, our advice to leaders is to be absolutely clear about your expectations of what TAs can and cannot do, and what you want them to achieve, if and when they are deployed to lead classes.

Be deliberate in your choice of the individual(s) to whom you assign this role. We have seen some schools assign a pair of TAs to lead a class, so that they can support one another.

We often hear that leading classes will not be something every TA in every school will wish to do; it takes a particular level of confidence and skills set to command a class of 30 pupils, especially if the culture of behaviour and/or respect for adults in the school is not all it could be. TAs we have spoken to as part of our research describe the damage to their confidence sustained by comments from pupils that undermine their authority and position; for instance: 'You're not a proper teacher'. Robust training and on-going supervision for TAs deployed to cover classes is therefore essential, and could be developed via opportunities for TAs to co-teach with a teacher.

You could consider developing a specific TA role along the lines of a cover supervisor to take on lesson cover and/or PPA cover more or less full time.

Case study

This case study comes from another school we worked with (not one of our five MITA Journeys schools).

The TAs described a common tendency for SLT to pull them away from intervention sessions in order to cover short notice teacher absences. The TAs expressed understandable frustration at the consequences these interruptions had on the coherence and consistency of the delivery of interventions, and the impact on pupils. TAs also felt compromised, insofar as they had to do as SLT directed. Another factor that contributed to TAs' anxieties was the tightness of their time-tables; there were very few gaps in the week where they could deliver any intervention sessions that were missed due to cover.

Conversations with the TAs revealed that they tended to view their timetables as a to-do list, and they experienced feelings of failure when they could not do what their timetable specified. They felt that they let children down. The leadership team was dismayed by this situation and explored alternative arrangements. The school redeployed one TA as a dedicated cover supervisor. A rolling bank of short tasks was compiled that the cover TA could pick up on the occasions when she was not needed for cover. These tasks were considered droppable should last-minute cover be required (e.g. putting up displays). The other TAs were soon freed from the sense that they were letting children or teachers down by not getting through the day's tasks, and the cover TA thrived, as this role played to her strengths and abilities as an effective interim classroom leader.

When the teacher is teaching

A question we are frequently asked on the topic of classroom deployment is: what can TAs do when the teacher is teaching the whole class? Behind this query is the concern that for lengthy episodes TAs may be sat passively, just listening to the teacher deliver the lesson. We understand why school leaders wonder whether this 'dead time' could be used more constructively.

Our first message to leaders concerned about this matter is not to assume TAs are idle during these periods. These moments are vital for TAs who miss out on pre-lesson pre-paration: they 'tune in' to the teacher's classroom talk in order to get up to speed about the lesson content and tasks; they listen for and pick up on keywords, relevant questions and pedagogical techniques to use when working with pupils during the main learning task.

Approached this way, the central issue is how to ensure TAs are properly equipped and prepared for the lessons in which they support; achieving this is the focus of Chapter 7. Improving TAs' preparedness by using time *outside* of lessons frees up those passive periods *during* lessons for other purposes. Evidence shows TAs can be passive for up to 20 minutes *per lesson* (Webster and Blatchford 2013). Multiply that by the number of lessons a week and the number of TAs in your school and you could be looking at hours of time that could be spent actively supporting teaching and learning.

Having TAs share part of the lesson input can have notable benefits. For example, when the TA collates answers or ideas and writes them up on the whiteboard, it allows the teacher to maintain eye contact with the room. This is, of course, useful for spotting any pupils who are having difficulty understanding the concept or task, and for responding to any off-task or inattentive behaviour the teacher would otherwise have missed with their back turned. It also makes the TA more visible to the pupils with whom they tend to spend less time (i.e. higher attainers), challenging perceptions about which pupils the TA is in the classroom *for*, and raising the TA's profile and their sense of value and worth.

We note that not all TAs will have the confidence to step into this role immediately, and not all teachers will want to co-teach every lesson. There will be occasions when it is not practical or necessary to have two adults at the front of the class. However, we believe it is something that schools can work towards in order to expand pedagogical capacity.

Teachers could constructively use teaching input time to ask TAs to collect useful information for them via informal observation. TAs could note responses from pupils and keep a record of pupil–teacher interactions in order to inform assessment for learning, or provide information on how pupils engage and interact with specific areas of lesson content. Such nuanced feedback can be helpful for class teachers who may miss these subtle behaviours whilst they are in the flow of teaching.

The key to ensuring that TA time is optimised while the teacher is teaching is for the teacher to clearly communicate what they want the TA to be doing in such moments prior to the start of the lesson.

A teacher–TA agreement

Breaking away from a model of deployment where TAs are assigned to specific pupils for long periods requires a more strategic and thoughtful approach to classroom organisation. School leaders are crucial here: encouraging the development of effective classroom partnerships. The MITA Journey schools developed teacher–TA agreements to help staff specify their coordinated, but differentiated, classroom roles. An agreement can bring clarity and consistency by setting out the ways in which TAs might contribute at various stages of a lesson, in such a way that they supplement, not replace, the teacher. You can find a version of the agreement template that the MITA Journeys schools used in Appendix 2. The same pro forma can be downloaded from our website.

It is worth noting that the secondary school from which our version was developed has various iterations of teacher–TA agreements reflecting different subjects. The teacher–TA agreement for science, for example, looks a bit different to the one used in food technology, but the underlying principles are the same. Teacher–TA agreements developed for use in different year groups in your setting could be similarly nuanced. Finally, we are particularly taken with the way the SENCO of this school describes these agreements as a way for teachers and TAs to establish a 'dance routine'.

Key recommendations on deploying TAs differently

- Consider how teachers deploy *themselves* in lessons, in terms of the groups they tend to support most often. Are they spending sufficient time with the pupils who need high quality instruction the most?
- Consider additional classroom organisation strategies that do not require adult support; for example, peer-led group work.

- Ask yourself: will pupils accept TAs leading classes? Is the culture and climate in my school conducive to this kind of role?
- Be absolutely clear about the limitations of TAs deployed to lead classes. They are *not* teachers, so calibrate your expectations accordingly. Ensure teachers are clear on this too.
- Ensure the deployment decisions devolved to teachers (at the classroom level) are clearly framed and delineated within your school policy on TA deployment; set expectations and limits of what is acceptable. Your aim is to achieve consistency in decision-making.
- Consider how to use the TA in different parts of the lesson to expand pedagogical capacity. Codify roles in a teacher–TA agreement. These can differ by year group, class or subject.

TAs' conditions of employment and recruitment

Decisions about TAs' contracts and hours of work have a bearing on how TAs are deployed and opportunities for preparation and planning time with teachers (Blatchford, Russell and Webster 2012). As you review your deployment decisions, you may find that issues relating to the recruitment of TAs and their conditions of employment are also in need of attention. We find that many schools use the MITA process to reset the clock; raising the bar by setting minimum entry levels to each type of TA role, and applying more rigorous standards to the selection process.

The TAs who are currently in post may present you with some particular challenges. Following your review of roles, you may be unable to align some individuals with certain roles, and so some changes in deployment will be necessary.

As we have already noted, the process of reform may result in dispensing with certain roles that currently exist. You may find yourself in a position where some of the TAs in your school do not, at present, have the competencies to fill the roles you want to establish. Or some TAs may not wish to fulfil the role you have in mind. This will be a matter for the individual. We do not underestimate the fact there may be difficult choices involved in undertaking the systemic programme of restructuring we are advocating in this book. But as educationalists, we have to put the needs of pupils first. If redundancies are likely, we recommend you seek advice.

However, we stress it is the *roles* that are to be done away with, not the individuals who occupy them. In fairness to TAs, the role has historically grown around them and this has not been accompanied with the necessary support to help them adjust. This is why we strongly advocate a process of training to support TAs to grow into the new roles you create.

In support of this strategic approach to managing and organising TAs, and treating them as professionals in their own right, there is one further consideration worth mentioning here. We will consider a range of practical options in Chapter 7, but for now it is important to say that taking the matter of improving TAs' preparedness seriously will often necessitate changes to their working hours. You may need to extend TAs' working day at the start, the end or both, in order to create meeting time for teacher liaison, and this may be problematic for some individuals. Again, these are matters it will be up to individuals to deal with. TAs who accept this new arrangement are likely to require new or updated contracts of employment, starting from the next school year. For new recruits, the hours of work you wish to introduce can be made clear during the application process, so they are able to make an informed choice about whether they would be willing to accept the conditions of employment associated with the role.

Key recommendations on TAs' conditions of employment and TA recruitment

- Reset your approach to TA recruitment. Approach future recruitment of TAs differently by specifying entry-level qualifications or experience, and making expectations and the hours of work clear.
- These arrangements should be formally expressed in a job description and person specification. The new standards and expectations should be defined by, and set out in, the school's TA policy.
- Conditions of employment will need to be reviewed for existing TAs and for all future contracts, particularly those relating to changes to working hours.
- Make every effort to train TAs who are currently in post if they do not possess the full skills set required for the role in which you wish to deploy them.

Summary

In this chapter, we have considered alternative models for deploying TAs, mainly in a pedagogical capacity, which are consistent with the principle of supplementing, not replacing, the teacher. In the final chapter of this book, we discuss the impact our MITA Journeys schools reported of implementing these approaches, and of moving away from the less effective practices identified in the DISS project. We conclude this chapter by briefly noting that when schools that have undertaken the MITA programme dedicate time and effort to fundamentally rethinking TA deployment, they report that teachers make more informed and more efficient decisions about how to deploy TAs in lessons (e.g. triaging; co-teaching). As a result, pupils who are typically supported by TAs (e.g. lower-attaining pupils and those with SEND) experience *less* separation from the classroom, receive *more* input in-class from teachers (either individually or as part of a group), and their dependency on TA support is reduced.

Note

1 The Professional Standards for Teaching Assistants are not mandatory, but sit alongside the statutory standards for teachers and headteachers, and help to define the role and purpose of TAs, to ensure that schools can maximise the educational value and contribution of adults working with pupils. The standards can be downloaded at www.maximisingtas.co.uk/resources.php.

Chapter 6

TAs' interactions with pupils

Scaffolding for independence

Introduction

Few would disagree that the quality of verbal interactions between adults and pupils is at the heart of effective teaching and learning. This chapter focuses on the quality and nature of TA–pupil interactions; or as the wider pedagogical role model puts it: 'practice'.

The DISS project revealed how schools were largely unaware that TAs' interactions with pupils tended to focus on getting tasks completed – and getting them completed correctly. A comparison of TA–pupil and teacher–pupil talk, based on detailed transcripts of classroom recordings, showed for the first time how TAs tended to close talk down with closed questions and spoon-fed answers (Rubie-Davies et al. 2010; Radford, Blatchford and Webster 2011). TAs 'over-supported' pupils, doing more for them than was necessary. As we shall see, while there are extenuating factors that can explain why this happens, the cumulative effect of over-support and the less cognitively demanding nature of TA–pupil talk, is that some pupils end up, in effect, 'outsourcing' their learning to a TA.

Another key finding from the DISS project, based on systematic classroom observations, was that the one-to-one interactions pupils had with TAs were not only longer, but also more sustained and more interactive, compared to their interactions with teachers. Further observations highlighted a phenomenon we call 'stereo teaching'. This describes the effect of how intermittent talk from TAs to pupils during the teacher's whole-class input can effectively separate pupils from the teacher. A common scenario is where the TA sits alongside a pupil, usually to the side or the back of room. Oftentimes, this is justified on the basis that this helps the pupil to concentrate. Yet, the unintended consequence of this is that the pupil hears two adult voices, rather than one; both very often saying the same thing – hence the stereo effect. This, if anything, makes it harder for the pupil to follow what the teacher is saying.

It was also very common to observe TAs not leaving much thinking or response time following a question. This seemed to occur as frequently as when a teacher asked a question (usually to the class as part of their whole-class input) as it did when it was the TA doing the asking.

Overall, TAs' interactions with pupils could be broadly characterised as *reactive*, because – unlike teachers, who guide lessons with planned learning aims in mind – TAs routinely respond to the needs of the pupils and the tasks in the moment. The difference between teachers' and TAs' subject and instructional knowledge was also evident in the classroom recordings, as TAs' explanations were found, on occasion, to be inaccurate or misleading (albeit unintentionally). Both of these factors are related to another mitigating factor, which is the focus of our Chapter 7: the lack of preparedness many TAs experience day-to-day. The less effective types of talk we hear from TAs is indicative of a wider story about how their role is designed and defined. This underscores a point we have keenly emphasised throughout this book, that almost everything about what TAs do in the classroom, and the impact it has (or does not have), is the result of decisions made (or not made) *about* them. The imagery of TAs being akin to the mortar in the brickwork, which we used in the Introduction, is quite potent here, because it is also illustrative of how TAs operate within the gaps; for example, by providing additional differentiation on the hoof because the task the teacher has set has not been sufficiently targeted to the needs of learners with SEND. This speaks to how a lack of clear direction from the teacher and a lack of liaison between teachers and TAs regarding explicit expectations can compound the situation. Mitigating common problems with planning and preparation is the focus of our next chapter.

On the basis of the evidence from the DISS project and subsequent research by ourselves and colleagues on TAs' interactions (Radford, Bosanquet, Webster and Blatchford 2014; Radford, Bosanquet, Webster, Blatchford and Rubie-Davies 2013), it is hard to avoid the view that schools tend not to know how to make the best use of the extended, more frequent interactions TAs have with pupils. It is not difficult to see how lower quality interactions play a part in affecting not only learning outcomes, but also the development of independence.

At the heart of the MITA process is the effort to reverse this situation: to ensure that what TAs say to pupils, how they say it, and when they choose to intervene, forms the basis of a new type of practice for TAs, which recasts their role as helping pupils to help themselves. As such, it is consistent with, and probably the best exemplification of, the third recommendation contained in the EEF guidance (Sharples, Webster and Blatchford 2018): 'use TAs to help pupils develop independent learning skills and manage their own learning'.

Some important questions to ask about TA–pupil interactions

- How much do you already know about the nature and quality of TAs' interactions with pupils?
- Do you attempt to monitor TAs' talk with pupils; for example, their use of questions?
- How would you respond if you discovered TAs frequently provided pupils with answers, or misled them (albeit unintentionally) with inaccurate information?

Professional identity

As we hinted at above, there are extenuating factors that help to explain *why* TAs' interactions with pupils are characterised by things like over-supporting and stereo-teaching. Before we proceed much further, it is important to understand what these factors are and how they have arisen, because they talk to wider matters that schools need to address in the holistic effort to improve the use of TAs, and with it, pupil outcomes.

Our concern, as we expressed in Chapter 2, is that despite the significant growth in our TA workforce, and in spite of universal agreement about their positive value, the education system has never resolved the fundamental question of defining their role and contribution. Because this ambiguity persists, so too do questions about their status in schools. If we are uncertain about the specific contribution we want TAs to make to learning, and how this relates, directly and/or indirectly, to pupil outcomes, how can we know what we are trying to maximise, and how? Crafting a compelling and creditable answer to this dilemma is central to addressing the impact question.

What we are talking about here, at least in part, is 'professional identity'. We use this term to describe the way in which we define ourselves in relation to our work, and the meaning we ascribe to the work we do. We define ourselves by what we do and why we do it. An individual's day-to-day practices, routinised and honed, and the meaning attached to these practices, are the building blocks of professional identity. Whether you work in a factory, a shop, an office, a hospital or a school, professional identity helps you, an individual, to find your place in the overall 'work machine' and locate your specific contribution to the organisation's chief mission. It is reported that on his first visit to NASA in 1962, President John F. Kennedy asked a janitor what he did for the space agency. 'I am helping to put a man on the moon', he replied confidently. The story is an urban legend, but it makes a palpable point: a professional identity is a key source of pride and purpose in what one does for a living.

Professional identity is also conspicuous when it is absent. Without a clear sense of belonging or that our contribution is valued by our employer, we can feel uncertain, devalued, demotivated, overlooked, disillusioned, lost and vulnerable. These visceral, human emotions are like a void that must be filled. If the organisation where an individual works fails to provide the contours within which a professional identity can be shaped, the individual will construct one themselves. Oftentimes, this self-constructed identity is formed unconsciously, and the effects are benign; that is, there is room for an individual to create a professional identity that does not interfere or inhibit the aims, performance or outputs of the organisation.

A decades-long policy vacuum relating to the role of TAs (see Chapter 2) puts them very much in the category of workers that can feel impelled to construct their own professional identity. Before we expand on this, there is a wider contextual element that we ought to acknowledge. The last decade was defined by recession and austerity. Many people working in the public sector lost their jobs as services, and investment in them, were downgraded. As with professional identity, the feeling of having at least some job security is important to us psychologically, in terms of our well-being and our sense of worth. Feelings of anxiety thrive under the precarious and pressurised conditions cause by an economic downturn. This can in turn, consciously and unconsciously, affect an individual's workplace performance, and in extremis, drive some to develop protective behaviours, such as constructing and projecting to leaders and decision-makers a unique usefulness to insulate oneself from possible redundancy.

The significance of a professional identity to TAs, and the perilous uncertainty provoked by a persistent fear for their income and employment, are central to explaining why we think TAs 'over support' pupils. As a form of practice, over-support is an overt way of making oneself appear indispensable. Two TAs from MITA Journeys schools summed it up thus:

> I think if you're standing there and you're not talking to a child or helping them with work, you felt like you weren't doing your job properly... There's been so much in the news and everything about TAs and schools getting rid of them... It's almost like you've really got to prove your worth and make sure that you are almost

indispensable, I suppose. I think you do that, don't you, because you think that's the best way to support the child.

TA (Crestwood)

I used to think that it reflected badly on me if that child hadn't produced any work.

TA (Alver Valley)

The ensuing series of unintended consequences of this will by now be clear. Over-support can create the illusion that certain pupils in the class need more help than perhaps they actually do. Because the continual presence of and interjections from a TA crowd out the opportunities for pupils to experience and develop independence, the teacher may believe they are further behind their peers or age-related expectations than is the case. The situation is further compounded where some pupils cultivate a learned helplessness.

This, what we might call 'self-fulfilling prophecy', has its origins in the long history of employing and deploying an individual TA to support a pupil with SEND on a one-to-one basis. The TA's employment and the inclusion of the child with a Statement (latterly an EHCP) became inextricably tied to one another. TAs are commonly deployed through higher needs funding or responsively to act as the means by which a child, whose needs do not neatly fit with the school's approach to teaching and learning, can be included. The professional identity and role of one-to-one TAs can unintentionally be defined by this difference. Furthermore, any unconscious effort to continually demonstrate that the pupil requires on-going support creates a kind of stasis. This may protect the TA's position, but it is at the cost of the child's educational and social development.

It is important to reiterate that we are *not* saying that TAs do any of this on purpose; that, in our view, is categorically *not* the case. We must recognise that, just like teachers, TAs' practice is driven by a compassionate and nurturing instinct. They do not want to see the children with whom they have formed strong bonds to fall further behind, and they can put pressure on themselves to ensure they keep up; all the more so if they feel that those pupils are getting overlooked by the teacher. The problem is that this manifests itself in less-than-helpful practices, such as stereo-teaching, spoon-feeding, and completion and correction.

We do believe, however, it is essential to bring these issues out into the open, and to recognise the full landscape of influences that shape TAs' role and impact. Now that we have, let us switch attention to where we go from here.

TAs as scaffolders of learning: A distinctive and transformational role

We believe there is a strong, evidence-rich case for developing a distinctive and transformational role for TAs, which can also be the basis for forging a professional identity. This role is centred on TAs' talk, and it maximises the unique opportunities they have for extended interaction with pupils. In short, the role for TAs that we have in mind seeks to replace the ineffective practices we listed above (stereo-teaching, spoon-feeding, etc) with more productive and purposeful types of talk, which can drive learning forward by reinforcing pupils' independent learning behaviours.

Since TAs frequently work with small groups and individuals, they are in the unique position of being able to monitor the step-by-step progress pupils make towards achieving learning goals. From this vantage point, TAs can provide immediate feedback and give targeted support with the parts of tasks pupils find difficult. This form of scaffolding, designed and calibrated specifically for TAs, is the key to ensuring pupils become able to work more independently.

Effective scaffolding ensures pupils are fully engaged in the task and learning potential is maximised. It also ensures that, over time, pupils develop the capability to carry out tasks with less or no support and have the confidence in themselves to attempt more challenging tasks. The scaffolding process encourages pupils to think of strategies they can use to solve the problem for themselves. We refer to this as 'knowing what to do when you do not know what to do'. The TA's role in this is to provide the *least* amount of help first. This is in stark contrast to what was found in the DISS project, where pressure to complete tasks resulted in TAs correcting and supplying answers with little or no prompting from pupils.

Scaffolding is the key to providing a quality learning experience, and when carried out correctly, it leads not only to greater independence, but also to an improved ability to cope with learning challenges and setbacks (often referred to as 'resilience'). Long-term effects extend to pupils being more positively disposed to accepting failure as an inevitable and healthy part of learning, and developing a deeper engagement in, and appreciation of, learning for learning's sake.

On the basis of evidence from our own studies (Radford, Bosanquet, Webster, Blatchford and Rubie-Davies 2013; Radford, Bosanquet, Webster and Blatchford 2014) and our on-going work with schools in the MITA programme, we have found TAs can be highly effective when given a good understanding of the importance of scaffolding and a clear role as the scaffolder of pupils' learning. In this chapter, we draw on self-reported evidence from the MITA Journeys schools to describe the implementation and impact of a role for TAs, which is centred on scaffolding for learning.

The Teaching Assistant's Guide To Effective Interaction

As we explained in the Introduction, this book works hand-in-hand with our sister publication, *The Teaching Assistant's Guide To Effective Interaction: How to maximise your impact* (Bosanquet, Radford and Webster 2021). In the same way that this book underpins the MITA course for school leaders, *The Teaching Assistant's Guide...* is the basis for our Maximising the Practice of Teaching Assistants (MPTA) training. Both the book and the training provide TAs with the knowledge and tools to improve their practice in line with the aim of creating more independent learners.

Succinctly put, our advice to schools in relation to challenging and changing the practice component of the WPR model is to implement the guidance in *The Teaching Assistant's Guide...* In this chapter, we introduce the scaffolding process at the heart of our sister book, and provide some illustrative examples of how it can be used. As we have emphasised throughout this book, unlocking the potential of your entire TA workforce requires the vision and full backing of the leadership team. So, here we provide additional advice, which is not contained in *The Teaching Assistant's Guide...*, on what school leaders should consider following the introduction of this approach, in terms of implementing, embedding and sustaining new practice, and ensuring there is sufficient on-going support to TAs.

What is 'scaffolding'?

We start by defining the concept of 'scaffolding'. It is a word that has various meanings to various people, so let us be clear about how we use it both here and throughout *The Teaching Assistant's Guide*... Scaffolding is the process by which learners are helped to achieve learning goals and to be able to carry out tasks independently.

The term was first used by Wood, Bruner and Ross (1976) to describe the process of effective one-to-one tutoring. Since then, the idea has been applied more generally to other classroom contexts. Scaffolding describes the ways adults provide *structured help* so that a pupil can learn a new skill or concept. Scaffolding can only be provided by a competent or skilled other; that is, someone who already knows how to achieve a given learning goal. Scaffolding is characterised by the way in which the more competent person supports the learner by providing the *least amount of help* necessary at any one point in the process. Wood and Wood (1996) itemise three things that are required for effective scaffolding in the classroom, and all three underpin the approach we have developed specifically for TAs:

1   Close monitoring of the pupil's progress towards the part of the task being worked on
2   Support that constantly adapts to the needs of the pupil
3   The gradual handover of responsibility and control of the task from the person doing the scaffolding to the pupil.

We define and use scaffolding separately from similar terms like 'help', 'support' and 'differentiation'. For us, 'help' is too general a term to describe what a TA needs to do when working with a pupil. For some pupils, help means 'getting the TA to do the task for me'. This is clearly at odds with our aim of nurturing independence. 'Support' is also too vague. Though we take it to mean anything that enables the pupil to access the task *except* doing it for them, support may take the form of resources, such as a writing frame or multilink blocks. These things can form part of a scaffolding approach but are not, in themselves, scaffolding. 'Differentiation', as we are interpreting it here, is the process of designing learner-appropriate tasks, which are required *prior to* and *in order for* scaffolding to take place.

Scaffolding is not about modifying the task, but simplifying what the pupil has to do in order to carry it out. So the adult *allows* the pupil to attempt each part of the task by themself, but provides structured help for any parts they find difficult. As the pupil becomes more skilled, they should be given more parts of the task to perform, until they can eventually perform all aspects in sequence, independently.

Scaffolding can *only* be provided through interaction. This is also why it is not the same as help, support or differentiation. Throughout the scaffolding process, the focus is on encouraging the pupil to think of strategies they can use to solve the problem for themselves. To put it into a sentence, the TA's role is to help pupils to know what to do when they do not know what to do.

Why scaffolding?

Why craft a role and a professional identity for TAs around scaffolding? One reason is pragmatism. Given our starting point, it makes sense to work with the long-established patterns of deployment, which sees TAs assigned to support small groups of pupils and individuals for extended parts of the lesson. However, there is a more intrinsic justification. Scaffolding is the key to providing a quality learning experience. When carried out correctly, it leads to:

- *Greater independence*: pupils are able to plan the next steps, problem-solve and review what they have done. They are able to do these things because the TA has helped them to develop these skills over time.
- *The ability to cope with learning challenges and setbacks*: often referred to as 'resilience', pupils are more able to persist with a learning challenge by drawing on a range of problem-solving strategies. The safety net of support remains accessible when these strategies fail.
- *Developing a relationship with failure*: TAs often support vulnerable pupils who have an ingrained fear of failure. They are reluctant to attempt something for fear of getting it wrong, so reinforcing a perception of themselves as a poor learner. The skills of scaffolding can help pupils accept mistakes and failures as an inevitable part of learning and, indeed, as an opportunity to learn.
- *A deeper engagement in, and appreciation of, learning for learning's sake*: pupils view challenges as a way of improving their learning skills. Ultimately, there is much to gain from TAs helping to instil within pupils a reassuring sense that what is important is the learning process, rather than just getting the answer right or completing the task. Indeed, improved outcomes and grades are more likely when pupils have a grip on their learning processes and a language to describe it.
- *Accessing the teacher for support when needed*: pupils are confident about asking subject specialists (teachers) for specific help when they do not understand a concept or how to do a task. This is particularly important in secondary schools when TAs may not have the level of subject knowledge needed to answer technical questions, or access to TA support may be reduced. From the beginning of their school career, all pupils need to feel confident in asking the teacher for help, with TAs providing vital support in terms of helping pupils identify the particular problem (i.e. which bit they are stuck with) and to formulate specific questions.
- *Greater opportunities for peer interaction*: pupils can also develop confidence to ask their peers questions about learning, as well as teachers. Being able to talk to their classmates about learning and to compare and verify understandings are important skills to develop. TAs have a role in facilitating these exchanges.[1]
- *Less risk of stigmatisation*: some pupils, especially older ones, can feel stigmatised by having 'a constant adult helper', as it can make them look 'different' or 'less able' than others. When pupils have the skills and opportunities to work independently, accessing teacher and peer support in the same way as other pupils when they require it, their self-confidence grows. Also, as a result, TAs become invaluable as they can spread their support across the classroom, benefiting a greater number of pupils.

All of the above can be achieved by having a consistent approach to how TAs interact with pupils. Compare these outcomes with the impact of over-supporting, spoon-feeding and stereo-teaching. Instead of fostering dependence, TAs do the opposite: they build pupils' independence.

However, moving pupils to a point where they are able to work more independently is no overnight task. We have found that the time it takes to see changes is contingent on how dependent pupils have become on adult support: the more dependent a pupil has become, the more resistant they are likely to be to solving problems by themselves, and to learning the skills of self-scaffolding.

The good news is that small changes are usually seen quickly and, once a pupil knows that the TA is going to be consistent in expecting them to work more independently, progress becomes self-sustaining. For some pupils, the journey to greater self-reliance is unlikely to be smooth; there will be backtracking and stalling along the way. But this is entirely consistent with the messiness and unpredictably of learning, which is not a linear process.

TAs that try our scaffolding techniques often report that pupils are able to do more independently than they initially thought they could. When the TA stops automatically providing the highest amount of support, the pupil responds by taking on more responsibility. Once pupils start to achieve as a result of their independent efforts, their self-esteem and confidence improves and they become keener to try things by themselves. We now know of classes where pupils challenge themselves to see how much they can do without support. The term 'comfortable struggle' is helpful here, as a TA from Crestwood explains:

> It's actually okay to see them struggle, you know, that comfortable struggle. It's okay to see that. It's okay for them to be pushed outside their comfort zone.
>
> TA (Crestwood)

A summary of scaffolding

Before we introduce our framework for scaffolding TA–pupil interaction, it is helpful to revise the key features of scaffolding. We have kept our summary below necessarily short, but you can find much more detail on the nature of scaffolding in *The Teaching Assistant's Guide…*

- Scaffolding happens only through interaction
- Scaffolding relates to the specific small goals (process success criteria) that a pupil is working on
- Scaffolding happens in the moment, in response to what a pupil has just said or done
- Scaffolding is informed by careful observation, diagnostic questioning and/or asking pupils to 'talk aloud' as they work
- Scaffolding can be more accurate and precise as more detailed information about the strategies a pupil is using becomes available
- Scaffolding relies on encouraging pupils to ask and answer the question, 'What do I do next?', effectively and routinely
- Scaffolding is defined by giving the least amount of support and consistently ensuring that pupils take as much responsibility for the task as they can.

Introducing the scaffolding framework for TA–pupil interaction

In Figure 6.1, we present our scaffolding framework. At the top of the framework is self-scaffolding, which offers the highest level of pupil independence. At the bottom of the framework is correcting. Correcting offers no pupil independence, because the adult is doing all the work. In this section, we will introduce each layer of the framework in turn, and then summarise its overall strengths in terms of bringing consistency

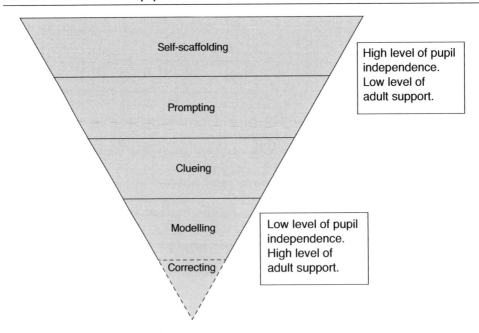

Figure 6.1 Scaffolding framework

and predictability to TA–pupil interactions. To illustrate what the layers of the framework look like in practice, we will relate each one to the task of writing an argument for or against school uniform, from the perspective of a fictional pupil called Reece.

It is important to note that the assumed starting point for using this framework is that the teacher has explained or modelled anything that is new to the class or about which they are not yet secure, *before* they try it for themselves. This applies specifically, of course, to the pupils the TA has been asked to work with.

Self-scaffolding

A pupil who is able to self-scaffold is an independent learner. Our aim for *all* pupils is for them to be more competent self-scaffolders. Pupils who self-scaffold are able to:

- Plan how to approach a task
- Problem-solve during the task
- Review the success of the task and how they approached it.

As a self-scaffolder attempting the writing task, Reece would be able to plan out what he needs to do. Deconstructing the key features of what needs to be included in his writing helps Reece to identify the process success criteria for this task (there is more on this in Chapter 7), which are:

- Writing a list of the advantages and disadvantages of having a school uniform
- Explaining whether he agrees or disagrees with having school uniform

- Providing reasons for his argument, with relevant examples
- Giving counter-arguments, for balance
- Explaining why he does not agree with the counter-arguments
- Summarising his overall argument.

If Reece hit a problem during the task, he would have strategies for solving it. For example, if he could not think of a counter-argument, he will know that he could ask a peer. As he proceeds with his writing, and once he has finished, Reece is able to review his work against the success criteria for the task.

Prompting (or encouraging)

Prompting represents the first level of adult intervention, when a pupil is unable to self-scaffold their way to the accomplishment of one of the steps that comprise the overall task (in *The Teaching Assistant's Guide…* we refer to these sub-procedures by the child-friendly term 'mini-goal'). Providing a prompt means saying or doing something to *encourage* the pupil to draw on their own knowledge of what to do when they do not know what to do. Prompting does not give any additional information or help.

Remaining quiet is actually a powerful prompt in itself, as extra thinking time is sometimes all that is needed. In Chapter 1 we explored the pressures that can lead TAs to focus on correction and completion, taking an active role in closing gaps to hurry along learning. By saying nothing, we are challenging this model by providing pupils with both the expectation and a non-pressurised space in which to work. Non-verbal prompting, or 'wait-time', works best when it is done consistently, across a class (e.g. waiting up for to five seconds) or for an individual pupil (e.g. all adults who support Reece allow him a seven second count, allowing him space to think about and share his own ideas). A specific time and count sets an explicit expectation, both on the pupil (least help first; no-one is going to supply the answer) and on the adult (to ensure consistency of approach).

If remaining silent for a period does not work, the TA would need to say something to encourage the pupil, but which avoided giving any idea of the strategy the child needs to use. In the case of our example, the TA could prompt Reece to think of an appropriate strategy from the ones he knows by saying something like:

- 'What do you need to do first?'
- 'What is your plan for structuring your writing?'

Prompting can be supported by visual aids, such as checklists. These can be specific to the task, or more general. Reece's list of key features of what to include in his writing (above) provides a useful example. The TA can then use a gesture prompt, such as pointing at the checklist, to support Reece to think some more about how to move forward.

Clueing

Sometimes pupils have the strategies or knowledge they need to solve the problem locked in their minds, but they find it difficult to recall them. A clue gives a child a hint in the right direction and puts them back on the road to independence. As we have described it, clueing sounds a bit like prompting; so what is the difference? Think of it this way: a prompt does not give any information or direct help, whereas a clue gives specific information to help the pupil move forward. So, in our example, the TA might give Reece a clue (or clues) such as:

- 'What did the teacher do before she started her writing?' *The answer is write a list of advantages and disadvantages*
- 'Do you agree or disagree with having a school uniform? Why?' *The answer will provide the structure for the first section of writing*
- 'You have said that not wearing school uniform is more expensive. How much more expensive are normal clothes?' *The answer will help them to extend their writing*

TAs should start with a small clue and add additional clues, if needed. TAs can always supply a greater level of scaffolding with a slightly bigger clue each time, but they need to avoid giving too much help straightaway.

Modelling

When a skill or strategy is completely new to a pupil, it needs firstly to be modelled effectively by the teacher. If, after prompting and clueing a pupil is still unable to solve the problem, then re-modelling may be appropriate. Modelling should be targeted to a specific step in the learning where the pupil is struggling (e.g. extending an answer). It should be short, so it can be more easily retained and applied afterwards. It should also provide a simple commentary that the pupil can follow and then repeat to themselves as needed.

To continue with our example, the TA might offer the following explicit model:

I am going to model how I extend my answer [picks up whiteboard and pen]. I will write my disadvantage [writes 'Uniforms are more expensive'], add a connective [writes 'because'], and then continue my sentence with a reason to back up my opinion ['you have to buy them new from special shops']. Now you have a try, Reece [wipes whiteboard clean]

By letting Reece know that she is modelling for him, the TA is cueing him to pay attention, and making it clear that, having remodelled, the next step is that he has to have a go himself. Reece knows that the TA is not going to do the task for him (indeed, she erases her example), so he needs to make best use of the model provided. By narrating the process, the TA gives Reece a commentary that he can replay when it is his turn.

To reiterate, as modelling by the teacher is the starting point for the entire scaffolding process we describe here, it is essential that they explicitly model key techniques in their whole class input, so that TAs' practice is then consistent when supporting pupils.

Correcting

Correcting is simply providing the right answer or completing the task for the child. This requires no independent thinking on the part of the child and is to be strenuously avoided. TAs operating within this layer of the framework can (as it were) 'put words into the pupil's mouth', and so give the pupil the next sentence they could write. So, in our example, the TA might say:

> So, Reece, you have said you do not like having school uniform. Is that because it is not very fashionable?

It is important here though to recognise the role of language modelling. Sometimes the TA's response might sound like a correction, but it is *actually* working as a language model. For example:

> TA: You have said that you do not like having school uniform. Why not?
> REECE: Not very fashion.
> TA: It is not very fashionable? OK, so you can give that as a reason

The TA's response ('It is not very fashion*able*') might be considered as correcting Reece's response, but she is deliberately stressing the suffix required for the answer to make sense. Models such as this are important. For example, pupils learning English as an additional language, or those who have difficulty with speech and language, require language models more than most. The key is in knowing whether a pupil would be able to self-correct if prompted, or if they need a correct model in order to move on.

Consistency and predictability

There is unlikely to be anything about the scaffolding strategies that is unfamiliar to either you or your TAs. Indeed, its relatability and intuitiveness is one of its main strengths. While several TAs in our MITA Journeys schools remarked that techniques such as prompting and clueing were things they already did, they recognised and valued the second great strength of the framework: its procedural reliability. What we mean here is that the framework structures TAs' responses and allows for a consistency of approach. The reason why this matters so much is that it makes TAs' interventions more predictable from the pupil's point of view. This in turn means that pupils become familiar with their role in a routinised sequence of learning interactions, and the kinds of things they can expect a TA to say and do to ensure they retain the responsibility for their learning and for the task. The following comments from staff in MITA Journeys schools illustrate how the consistent application of the scaffolding framework had reset the expectations pupils had of the support they provided, and how this was beginning to show signs of impact.

> As we went through [the MPTA training], we were saying: 'Well, yeah, we already do that, we already do that'. But it made us reflect on how to structure [interactions], how to scaffold... Check ourselves, that we were actually doing what we should be doing... because we just do it automatically.
>
> TA (Laureate)

> I think they [the pupils] found it hard to cope with to start with. Over time, they're used to that now. They're used to thinking: 'OK. I need to listen to the teacher; I've got to get on, because if I turn around and look for support, you know, we're

just going to say: "Think about what you've just been told. What was the first thing that you need to do?"'

TA (Crestwood)

It's encouraging them to think for themselves. I think it's good that we've taken a step back... I think we've definitely made huge progress there. They're [pupils] organising themselves for learning and they're thinking for themselves.

TA (Alver Valley)

It has, I think, significantly helped our children; not just academically, but also in terms of their independence, their confidence, their ability to problem solve, to be able to just get on, and their focus, their concentration. And I really don't think it has made a huge difference to our workload.

Teacher (Cuddington Croft)

Implementing the scaffolding framework and embedding and sustaining practice

We know that historically TAs have little or no choice about the ways in which they are deployed. Given this context, and – as our work with schools often shows – that some TAs will latch on to and adopt new practices quicker than others, school leaders should be mindful that it may take time to reach a position where every TA has undone old habits and replaced them with effective scaffolding techniques. The way TAs in the MITA Journeys schools described learning to provide thinking time is a good example of this. As a TA at Cuddington Croft explained:

I was always, I fully admit, too quick to jump in. I wouldn't necessarily give them the answer, but then I might start the clueing. I've learned, especially with one girl in my class, that it just takes her that little bit longer to process... I do have to bite my lip, but invariably she gets it, and she gets the answer right. So, I think that's one of the really big things that has come out of the project, for me, is just learning to live with those silences.

As part of your planning to introduce new training into your setting, you will need to consider how it will be embedded and sustained. This is essential for building on the promise of any professional learning. Additional training, individualised coaching, ongoing support, and providing opportunities for staff to practise and reflect should be factored in to your wider, long-term implementation plan. While in this case we are mainly referring to TAs, teachers may also need support in adapting to new ways of working that encourage pupils to become independent learners.

Our experiences of working with and learning from schools that have undertaken training on the scaffolding approach has yielded numerous examples of strategies to ensure longevity. Below, we describe some of these useful ideas that you might like to consider for your setting.

Firstly, you need to ensure that all of your TAs and teachers are clear about the scaffolding language and strategies, so that they can be applied consistently. Then you need to extend this to the pupils. Consider providing pupils with some explicit instruction on self-scaffolding, and carefully explain how the TAs will hereon be supporting pupils' development of these skills. For some children, this is likely to challenge long-standing perceptions of what TAs are for. This is likely to be most relevant to pupils with SEND, and especially those with an EHCP, for whom greater independence is often a specific developmental goal, and also to those with the greatest learned helplessness. You will need to reset their expectations and potentially those of some parents. We know of schools that share the scaffolding approach with parents, and encourage them to use some simple strategies at home in order to reinforce what is happening in the classroom; for example, using a checklist to prompt the child about what they should pack in their school bag each day.

Secondly, you should consider how the self-scaffolding can be integrated with your current pedagogical approach. In some cases, self-scaffolding strategies will need to be calibrated to particular year groups. Schools involved in the Mobilise TA project across Lincolnshire adapted the scaffolding framework for use in early years settings and produced child-friendly versions of it for use in the different primary Key Stages. The online repository of these resources is worth exploring.[2] We know of some teachers that have turned the scaffolding framework into a large classroom display of various self-help strategies, to which pupils can instantly refer when they get stuck. The framework also provides a structure for collecting and providing feedback on learning (see box). We will return to this in the next chapter.

Teachers, then, play an important role in facilitating change, by recognising and planning in opportunities for pupil independence and the self-scaffolding strategies. Building new habits and routines for pupils requires us first to habituate practices for the adults that teach and support them. Educators intuitively know they should leave adequate wait time and ask questions more carefully. Many of the approaches we have discussed here are designed to set clear expectations for staff, as well as pupils.

MITA Journeys

Using the scaffolding framework as the basis for a feedback strategy

Several MITA Journeys schools described how TAs were tagging pupils' work with codes relating to the layers of the scaffolding framework. For example, they would write 'SS' to indicate where a pupil had self-scaffolded or arrived at an answer independently (regardless of whether it was correct) or worked without adult support. Similar codes were used to indicate where the TA had provided a prompt (P), a clue (C) or modelled something for the pupil (M). A teacher at Shirley Manor described how this practice evolved to become a more explicit, child-focussed feedback strategy:

> It was a kind of an organic process... [the pupils] started noticing the markings in the book and were asking teaching staff and TAs what it meant, and why they were getting these marks by their work. We then discussed it in staff meetings and decided it should be a transparent process; the kids should be aware of it. So then, we put it up on the wall and having that conversation with them as to what clueing means. What does a prompt look like? They're striving towards that independence themselves, because they know that the more assistance they need, the less independent they are.

Thirdly, and related to the point above, it is essential that you integrate self-scaffolding into any wider related initiatives you are running. We are referring specifically here to the shadow curricula that support the development of soft skills, such as growth mindset (popularised by Carol Dweck) alongside academic knowledge. Our scaffolding framework also neatly aligns with the development of metacognition and self-regulated learning, and specifically the guidance report the EEF have published on this topic (Quigley, Muijs and Stringer 2018). If your school has a whole-school learning initiative of this nature, it is essential that you involve TAs in it. Remember: whole school means whole *staff*.

Finally, you may need to consider appropriate target-setting and review for both pupils and TAs. For pupils with SEND, this can be integrated into your graduated approach. We know of schools where the target-setting and review process has been informed by the layers and language of the scaffolding framework. You should have good systems in place for monitoring what TAs are doing, too. This could include observation and giving feedback on how their interactions are impacting pupils' independence targets. Some of the MITA Journeys schools made the effective use of scaffolding skills a part of TAs' annual performance review (see box).

Establishing a form of soft accountability, together with the other implementation factors we have described in this chapter, are all helpful in providing the structure and framing we have argued is necessary for constructing a meaningful professional identity for TAs.

MITA Journeys

Linking scaffolding to professional development and performance review

Several MITA Journeys schools developed performance review targets for TAs relating to the scaffolding framework. In doing so, they monitored TAs' progress to improving and embedding effective practice on building pupil independence. It is important to say that this was done in a collegiate and supportive way, in the spirit of professional development, rather than hard-edged accountability.

Building on specific guidance in *The Teaching Assistant's Guide…* and the training relating to it that staff received, Alver Valley encouraged TAs to make a video recording of their interactions with one or two pupils. These were used as the basis for professional discussions in pairs. Perhaps understandably, the TAs were apprehensive about recording and sharing their practice at first. Jill Roseblade (Headteacher) and Kate Russell (Assistant Head and SENCO) recognised that in order for this idea to work, they needed to trust the TAs and to remove any perceived threat:

> They worried that we were going to use those videos to pull out things where their practice is not great. I said: 'No, the videos are for your use only. It's to share with your partner, and they will pick out the things that they think you can work on'. It's about peer relationships and about working together, but not with me breathing down their necks.

After discussing practice, the TAs wrote an action plan, itemising just two or three areas of improvement, and then met again to review progress several weeks later. Despite some initial, and not uncommon, anxieties about watching oneself on video, Jill and Kate reported that the TAs were beginning to warm to the benefits of recording and reviewing their practice:

> The first couple of times when they had a go, they all said: 'We don't like doing it, we hate it.' But then, it shifted and people were keen... well, not keen, but they were happier! I think they could see themselves moving forward with what they were actually watching, how they practised at it in the classroom. They were able to see the benefits of recording themselves.

Key recommendations on implementation, embedding and sustaining practice

- Position the goal of ensuring TA–pupil interactions promote independence as central to your intentions, aims and implementation of MITA.
- Craft a professional identity and distinct role for TAs around scaffolding and fostering pupil independence.
- Be transparent and explicit about your aims and aspirations for MITA, and ensure these align with and complement other initiatives.
- Ensure that every member of the school community (including parents) are clear about the scaffolding approach and the language of the scaffolding framework.
- Monitor and support TAs as they develop new scaffolding skills. Provide guidance, coaching and opportunities to practise.
- Encourage TAs to become reflective practitioners and provide opportunities for TAs to have professional dialogue
- Allow time for new practices to bed in and to take effect.

Summary

In this chapter, we have argued for creating a distinctive and transformational role for TAs as scaffolders of learning, which has the added advantage of bringing clarity, purpose and identity to their job. We discussed the concept of scaffolding and introduced a framework to support TAs in their interactions with pupils. Using the experiences of the MITA Journeys schools, who received training and support to transform the nature, quality and purpose of TAs' talk as part of the wider MITA programme, we explored the broader implementation factors that enable this work to thrive. Within these settings, school leaders, TAs and teachers articulated the benefits of this work, and identified emerging signs of impact, which included TAs putting a greater emphasis on learning – *not* task completion – and timing and pacing interactions to allow pupils more time to think and respond, and giving them space and opportunities to work independently.

Notes

1 *The Teaching Assistant's Guide…* contains a chapter on how TAs can facilitate groups and support group work.
2 The Mobilise TA project resource bank is available at https://mobilise.kyrateachingschool.com/resources

Chapter 7

The preparedness of TAs
Improving their readiness for the role

The persistent problem of preparedness

How well prepared are your new and recently qualified teachers? Are they adequately prepared to teach across all the curriculum subjects? How well has their training prepared them to meet the learning needs of pupils with SEND, and those who underperform academically? What about the level of their day-to-day preparation? Are you aware of how well your new teachers are prepared for each day's lessons? Are you confident their plans are clear, detailed and matched to the learning needs of their pupils?

Now replace the references to 'new and recently qualified teachers' in the questions above, with 'teaching assistants', and ask yourself the same questions.

Preparedness – that is: (i) opportunities for professional development; and (ii) the opportunities for, and quality of, planning and feedback between teachers and TAs – has been a consistent theme in research on TAs. In fact, it is the lack of such opportunities that makes preparedness something of a persistent problem.

In terms of professional development, three biennial teacher surveys conducted over the life of the DISS project revealed how little exposure teachers had to training on how to manage and organise the work of TAs. Each survey wave found that around 75 per cent of teachers reported having had no such training (Blatchford, Russell and Webster 2012). The persistent lack of pre-service training for teachers in England has been routinely captured in regular surveys of newly qualified teachers (NQTs), conducted for the Department for Education. The most recently available survey (Ginnis et al. 2018) found that knowing how to deploy TAs effectively was one of the aspects of their initial teacher training (ITE) for which NQTs felt least prepared. Just 54 per cent felt secure on this area of their practice. This is consistent with the previous survey in which NQTs ranked their confidence of working with TAs at 52 per cent (Pye et al. 2016).[1]

It is worth noting that NQTs rank their confidence in teaching pupils with SEND at a similarly low level. These surveys found that just over half (52–53 per cent) felt secure on this area of their practice. Such findings are in keeping with the way coverage of SEND has been consistently undervalued in ITE over several decades (Hodkinson 2019).

There has been little progress in improving TAs' access to professional learning, too. In the DISS project, we found that while training for TAs was broadly described as good and worthwhile, opportunities were limited. Where TAs do receive training, it is usually on aspects of SEND (Webster and Blatchford 2017), and this, in turn, helps to perpetuate the separation effect we described in Chapter 5. This echoes the patchy picture of TAs' professional development described in a systematic review by Cajkler et al. (2007). While there are no centrally collected data on this topic (akin to the NQT survey), our experience of working with schools in the UK routinely reveals that training for TAs is inconsistent and something of a neglected area (see Chapter 3). While it is highly likely that this situation has been exacerbated by cuts to school funding, the exclusion of TAs from professional development opportunities is an issue that is as old as the role itself.

The second expression of preparedness concerns how TAs are prepared on a day-to-day basis for the typically instructional roles that they take on in the classroom. This too has been persistently problematic. One of the DISS project's key findings was that 75 per cent of teachers reported having no allocated planning or feedback time with the TAs they worked with. Communication between teachers and TAs was largely ad hoc; conversations took place during lesson changeovers, before and after school, and during break and lunch times, and so, for the most part, relied on the goodwill of TAs. Many TAs reported feeling under-prepared for the tasks they were given. With little or no time to talk with teachers beforehand, TAs described how they 'went into lessons blind'. They had to 'tune in' to the teacher's delivery in order to pick up vital subject and pedagogical knowledge, and information and instructions relating to the tasks they supported pupils with.

We have found the same situation in our research ever since the DISS project; specifically, the Effective Deployment of Teaching Assistants (EDTA) project (Webster, Blatchford and Russell 2013) and a large-scale observational study of the educational experiences of pupils with a Statement in primary schools (Webster and Blatchford 2013). Perhaps unsurprisingly then, prior to undertaking the MITA programme, staff in MITA Journeys schools described familiar scenarios playing out across their classrooms, with predictable consequences:

> It's awful coming into a class and not knowing what you're doing and thinking, 'I'm not sure what's going on here'.
>
> TA

> Teachers were always involved in the planning, never the TAs. It wasn't that teachers couldn't do it [involve TAs]; it's not that they didn't want to. They had never considered it before.
>
> Headteacher

As we described in Chapter 1, the EDTA project was the action research project that led to MITA. One of the primary school TAs who participated in that project summed up the day-to-day preparedness predicament thus:

> There is an assumption that you should just know. You're to come into a classroom, you listen to the 20 minutes of teaching, and from that − if you didn't know, you should know now. And then you're to feed it to the children. It's scary.

We use this quotation a lot in our work with schools, because it is so indicative of a common experience that will be familiar to many TAs. It neatly captures the persistent problem school leaders must seek to resolve in relation to going into lessons without sufficient preparation, and having to differentiate on the hoof; or, as the TA above refers to it, 'feeding' curriculum content to the children who, as we know, struggle more than most to access it. Little wonder she describes this as 'scary'.

In Chapter 5, we stated that decisions about deployment provide the starting point from which all other decisions about TAs flow. Having established what roles you want TAs to perform and how they should be deployed and interact with pupils (see Chapter 6), you will need to consider the appropriate forms of preparation needed for them to be successful. In this chapter, we consider the decision-making needed to ensure TAs are fully prepared for the work school leaders and teachers ask them to do. This tallies with recommendation four of the EEF guidance (Sharples, Webster and Blatchford 2018).

It should be said that although improving TAs' preparedness has inevitable consequences for teachers' preparedness – that is, how well they are able to manage and work with TAs – the purpose of this chapter is to offer guidance on how to improve the preparedness of TAs, rather than teachers. Our brief summary of salient findings from recent research above illustrates how the issue of working with TAs has not been given enough attention in ITE. Our view is that ITE providers must address this deficit more fully; but clearly this matter is beyond the scope of this book. For school leaders, the main message is this: if you take seriously the need for teachers to plan, manage and evaluate the work of TAs successfully, you need to provide teachers with further training opportunities to help them achieve this. We highlight this throughout this chapter where relevant.

Some important questions to ask about teachers' training

- In your judgment, have your teachers been adequately prepared to work with and organise the TAs that work regularly in their classrooms?
- Have your teachers been adequately trained to share or delegate teaching with/to TAs?
- Do you know what training your teachers have had in order to support the needs of pupils with SEND, and what gaps they may have in their knowledge?

The results of your audit will inform decisions about how to deploy TAs in appropriate roles. Once decided, you need to consider how you train TAs for pedagogical roles and non-pedagogical roles, and put in place processes and systems to support their day-to-day preparation.

Preparing TAs for non-pedagogical roles

Supporting teachers

Training

As we set out in Chapter 5, perhaps the most extreme expression of a non-pedagogical TA role is one in which they do not routinely interact with pupils. If you have chosen to create roles for any of your TAs that help teachers with their routine admin tasks, it may be necessary to offer forms of training. Some tasks, like data entry, will require using specific software. TAs with an ostensibly behaviour management role in classrooms would, of course, require targeted training in specific techniques, such as de-escalation, and which have a consistent fit with your school's behaviour policy.

Day-to-day preparation

Daily preparation for TAs in non-pedagogical roles is unlikely to require regular meetings between teachers and TAs. Most of what needs to be communicated can be done in fairly ad hoc ways or through written notes. For example, we are aware of some teachers who keep a 'jobs book' in which they maintain a list of tasks TAs can do during quieter moments.

In terms of the day-to-day preparation for TAs with a behaviour monitoring role, there will be a need for teachers and TAs to share information at the start and end of lessons. This might include, for example, whether any pupils have had a difficult morning or experienced trouble at home the night before, and may therefore be more likely to be volatile or fractious during the lesson. This type of role may have the effect of the TA engaging with some parents more regularly than the class teacher. Home-school diaries and regular morning meetings between TAs and parents are likely to be helpful in supporting school behaviour strategies, but it is important that the class teacher provides the feedback and retains responsibility for the overall approach.

The teacher will mostly be aware of the behaviour incidents that will need to be followed up after a lesson, should any occur. This, therefore, reduces the need for TA feedback after the lesson. Nonetheless, TAs should be encouraged to briefly report back any relevant information of which the teacher may not be aware before they leave the classroom.

Behaviour tracking approaches can help formalise this, by providing the TA with a more specific role and feedback cycle, which are part of, or aligned with, the whole school approach to behaviour. The TA could, for example, work with the school's behaviour or pastoral lead on a weekly cycle to review incidents or concerns, supervise school sanctions, agree which pupils to track, and target with specific programmes of support. On a pupil-specific level this could be as straightforward as a TA working with a pupil on their behaviour management plan (supporting specific targets and strategies), or collecting data using an ABC chart to record incidences of behaviour, with its antecedent and consequence. These data can then be analysed for patterns, identifying triggers, typical responses to certain events, etc. Such examples give clear definition and direction to the TA's role within a broader framework of behaviour management, intercedence and review.

Supporting pupils' physical and emotional needs

Training

TAs who support pupils with physical/mobility, visual or hearing impairments are likely to have already had particular training in appropriate techniques, such as handling or sign language. Following your review of roles, any TA deployed in such a capacity who has not had training will need to be skilled up or update their training.

As we noted in Chapter 5, TAs are well positioned to support pupils' emotional needs. TAs often have the appropriate characteristics (e.g. warmth and attentiveness) required for nurturing roles. However, these cannot be considered sufficient qualifications for supporting pupils with profound emotional difficulties, such as those who have experienced trauma in early childhood. You will need to ensure TAs are properly trained and qualified to take on nurturing or emotional support roles. Programmes delivered by Emotional Literacy Support Assistants (ELSAs) to support pupil wellbeing, for example, train TAs to use basic counselling skills (e.g. active listening and problem clarification) to guide conversations. It is advisable that anyone undertaking higher-level counselling work receives appropriate supervision from a suitably qualified person. ELSAs, for example, receive regular professional supervision from an educational psychologist. Complex cases, however, must be referred to mental health professionals.

Day-to-day preparation

TAs who support pupils with physical needs need to be prepared in similar ways to TAs in pedagogical roles (more of which later). They may need access to teachers' lesson resources in advance, in order to make specific modifications; for example, making enlarged photocopies of worksheets for pupils with a visual impairment. Any prior knowledge of lesson content will help TAs to prepare in advance; for example, how they will convey particular information or concepts to pupils with a hearing impairment.

As with the daily preparation for TAs in behaviour monitoring roles, it will be necessary for TAs who support pupils with physical needs to share some information with teachers at the start and end of the lesson, regarding, for example, the organisation of the lesson and the classroom: will the TA need to make any particular modifications in order to ensure the pupil can access the lesson? For pupils with emotional needs, TAs can once again inform teachers at the start of the lesson of any factors that may affect an individual's engagement and behaviour during the lesson. In both cases, feedback from TAs at the end of the lesson will be necessary to inform future lesson planning.

It is for you and your SLT to make the forms of day-to-day preparation and feedback described above obligatory throughout the school. This expectation can be written into your school policy on TA deployment. Routine feedback will enable teachers to become more informed about how pupils respond to their lessons and their teaching strategies, and allow them to reflect meaningfully on their practice.

Key recommendations on preparing TAs for non-pedagogical roles

- Ensure TAs with behaviour management roles receive thorough training. Make sure this role and the techniques TAs use are consistent with school policy and structures regarding behaviour management.
- TAs who support pupils' physical and social development should receive formal training and hold the necessary qualifications to perform these roles. Refer complex cases to mental health professionals.
- Ensure teachers brief TAs at the start of lessons and that there are mechanisms for obtaining feedback.
- Identify a set of particular tasks (e.g. modifying resources) TAs can do to help teachers prepare for meeting the needs of pupils with physical or sensory needs in classrooms.

Preparing TAs for pedagogical roles

Training

The outcome of a staff audit will show the range of qualifications and skills held by your TAs, and highlight any gaps you may need to fill. In light of this, you should consider training to raise the quality of TAs' contributions to pupils' learning for those deployed in pedagogical roles.

Seek to implement a comprehensive and coherent whole-school strategy to address these gaps. As we have made clear, taking steps to change TAs' levels of preparedness should not preclude efforts to address the training needs of teachers. Both are important, of course, but what we mean by this is that you must avoid skilling-up TAs as a proxy for addressing gaps in teachers' pedagogical knowledge and skills, especially when it comes to meeting the needs of those with SEND.

Our general view is that school leaders should focus their attention on upskilling their TAs in a way that is consistent with supplementing, not replacing, the pedagogical role and responsibilities of the teacher. In the previous chapter, we outlined a case and a process for improving TAs' interactions with pupils in line with this view, in terms of scaffolding for independence. Indeed, recalibrating the role of TAs around this particular function was precisely what our MITA Journeys schools opted to do. We strongly recommend you consider doing likewise by considering training on effective classroom talk using this book's sister publication, *The Teaching Assistant's Guide to Effective Interaction*, which builds considerably on the coverage of Chapter 6.

Developing TAs' subject and pedagogical knowledge

Given this supplementary function, it follows that TAs' subject and pedagogical knowledge does not need to be at the same level as that of your teachers. However, TAs do need to be secure on certain fundamentals if they are to be effective in their role.

Much of what TAs require in terms of developing both their subject and pedagogical knowledge can be achieved through in-house training. You could, for example, introduce regular informal 'mini-tutorials' for TAs, where teachers can brief them on topic information or technical processes (see MITA Journeys box), or set up a series of collaborative enquiries to improve practice (see Case study box).

MITA Journeys

Boosting TAs' subject knowledge

The introduction of Maths Mastery at Laureate provided the opportunity to road-test teacher–TA planning sessions, which incorporated introducing and revising new pedagogical techniques. One teacher described the value of having quality time with the year group TAs in order to prepare for maths lessons:

> In terms of Maths Mastery, when we've got new concepts that we've not taught before, to be able to have that time together, I found it really valuable. We'll look at a Maths Mastery video and talk about how we're going to teach it the next week, or that next unit. It's having that time. It's not just as you fly past each other kind of conversation. I think it shows the importance of the TAs' input.

Case study

A Lesson Study approach

This case study comes from a primary school that participated in the EDTA project.

Lesson Study describes a peer observation technique, which has origins in Japanese education. Adapted for the purposes of developing teaching practice among teacher–TA teams, staff in one school worked collaboratively in small groups to discuss learning goals and plan a 'research lesson'. Members of the group either delivered or observed the lesson, then discussed and revised for a second iteration, with observers and deliverers swapping roles. The outcomes (e.g. what went well, not so well, etc.) were later shared with all school staff.

The three teachers and three TAs in each year group planned and delivered a research lesson. Importantly, colleagues did not judge or grade one another's performance in the lesson. Instead, with Lesson Study, the focus is on groups or specific pupils and their learning journey through the lesson. The Deputy Headteacher reflected on this as professional development tool:

> As they have all planned the lesson together, it is much easier to discuss where things maybe have not worked. TAs have found it very useful to observe other colleagues and learn from each other's practice.

A related issue is that of moving to a class in a different Key Stage. Some form of induction is often required when moving to a new or unfamiliar part of the school, especially for less experienced TAs. TAs at one of our MITA Journey's schools developed a useful system for helping colleagues to familiarise themselves with the curriculum, assessment and expectations within each year group (see box below).

Of course, it might not be possible or practical to meet all training needs for TAs through in-house training. External training provision may be necessary, particularly in preparing TAs to support and interact with pupils with particular types of SEND and delivering particular curriculum interventions (see Chapter 8). Continuing professional development that leads to qualifications and accreditation should be available and will formalise the acquisition of new skills, as well as enhancing TAs' confidence and self-image.

MITA Journeys

Learning support folders

TAs at Cuddington Croft had compiled 'learning support folders' for each class. These contained information about the year group, examples of pupil work at the expected standard for that year group, exemplar marking and feedback, notes and observations from the incumbent TA, and any other useful documents. Any teachers moving to a new class were encouraged (and willing) to take the class folder home over the summer holidays. As one TA explained the idea was:

> ...to make it like a little 'bible' for that year group to hand over to the new TAs, so that they could familiarise themselves, and be ready to hit the ground running in September.

Training for TAs who lead classes

In Chapter 5, we explored the role of TAs leading classes as part of arrangements to release teachers for PPA and/or to cover short-term teacher absence. If you choose to deploy TAs to lead classes, you need to ensure they have the necessary skills. Again, a programme of in-house training should be developed to ensure TAs are given quality training from experienced teachers in classroom management skills. The role and the training will be framed by the expectations set out in the school policy on the appropriate use of TAs to work in place of teachers. Monitoring and mentoring should also feature as crucial elements of the training programme, so TAs are supported in the early stages of their role.

Key recommendations for preparing TAs with pedagogical roles

- Consider cost-effective in-house approaches to developing TAs' subject and pedagogical knowledge (e.g. mini-tutorials), so they are more able to promote thinking and learning through their interactions with pupils.
- Ensure TAs that lead classes receive training in classroom management and are supported by wider school systems.
- Consider the potential of informal training methods, such as peer observation. Identify a specific area of focus and encourage reflective practice and discussion.

Induction and performance review

Induction

We have heard anecdotally of TAs receiving highly questionable forms of induction consisting of little more than reading pupils' individual educational plans or EHCPs, or looking through resource packs and materials from intervention programmes. Similarly, teachers have told us that even if they received some form of induction, it rarely included anything substantive on what the school expected from them in terms of TA deployment.

Our view is that all newly appointed TAs and teachers (including trainees) should receive a full induction into the school's expectations and practices relating to the work of TAs. Your school policy on TA deployment is a useful vehicle for structuring induction and training around what the school expects from new teachers, and what new TAs can expect from teachers, in terms of being adequately prepared and deployed for pedagogical tasks.

Valuable models of school induction we have encountered include opportunities for new TAs to shadow experienced and effective TAs. If this is extended to new teachers as well, this form of shadowing can help new staff to have a better understanding of what the policy means in practice. Furthermore, through lesson observations, new appointees will be exposed to what the school regards as exemplary teacher–TA collaboration in lessons. New staff could sit in on teacher–TA planning and feedback meetings to see how lesson plans are used and shared, once again providing the opportunity for them to get familiar with the kinds of practice the school expects them to adopt. Once established, peer observation can help TAs feel valued, and encourage open and reflective practice.

One school we worked with implemented an induction process where new TAs spent the first two weeks of their appointment off-timetable, shadowing an experienced TA and having short meetings with key members of staff (e.g. the SENCO; the teacher in whose class they would work) to talk about the school's values, context, policies, curriculum, expectations, etc. The Deputy Headteacher who came up with this idea justified it on the basis that new TAs could 'hit the ground running' once in the classroom. Previously, inductions were informal, on-the-job, and essentially drawn out over four or five weeks, as a new TA learned about the job at the same time as trying to do it. Taking time to get it right from the start saved time in the long run and ensured TAs (especially those entirely new to the role) entered the classroom with more confidence.

Performance review and audit cycle

Of course, monitoring the work of new staff is not a one-off activity. New teachers and TAs will become part of the annual performance review process. Their performance, in terms of how they uphold or are supported by the school's policy on TAs, should form part of your overall evaluation of their performance. In particular, this will have greater implications for teachers than for TAs, as it is teachers' decision-making regarding TAs that is under scrutiny; with TAs' effectiveness reviewed in the context of these decisions.

Some of the self-evaluation processes we described in Chapter 4 can be used to help you audit and update your records on TAs' qualifications and training. A regular audit cycle is intended to maintain the identification of training needs, and school leadership teams should make provision for the necessary updating of staff's knowledge and skills. There should, of course, be room for collaboration here, too, with TAs able to nominate specific areas of their practice they want to improve. A sense of ownership over target helps with overall buy-in to the performance review process.

Key recommendations on induction and performance review

- Introduce a formal programme of induction for new teachers and TAs on TA deployment, structured around the school policy on TAs.
- Induction training could include the opportunity to shadow an experienced, effective TA, and maybe time off-timetable to acclimatise to the post and setting.
- Ensure new teachers and TAs receive support and guidance in the early stages of their appointment.
- Use the auditing tools to carry out an annual review of how the school policy is being implemented, and to identify and meet gaps in teachers' and TAs' knowledge and skills.

Day-to-day preparedness

School leaders and teachers do not need to be convinced of the need to provide opportunities for teachers and TAs to prepare for lessons and to feedback afterwards. But for many, it is the capacity to create this time that is the greatest practical barrier. We hear time and again from schools we work with in the MITA programme how the general busyness of schools and TAs' hours of work falling in line with the school day are impediments to creating liaison time for TAs and teachers, and to improving preparedness. We fully appreciate that creating meeting time has a financial implication. Indeed, the persistence of the preparedness conundrum can (at least in part) be explained by the ongoing pressures schools experience in relation to funding.

Nonetheless, we strongly encourage school leaders to see the need for some form of liaison as central to maximising the impact of TAs. Without opportunities to meet and discuss lessons with teachers, efforts to improve the contribution and value of your TA workforce will be undermined and potentially undone. As one Headteacher who participated in the MITA programme memorably put it: 'I started this process thinking I can't afford to create meeting time for teachers and TAs. But it wasn't long before I realised I can't afford *not* to create meeting time for teachers and TAs'.

Creating time for teachers and TAs to meet

In our experience, an early audit of current practice is a highly effective way of drawing out experiences and views concerning the opportunities for, and quality of, teacher–TA liaison. Practical problems are often brought to the surface, some of which you, as a leader, might predict, and others that you may not have foreseen. A common issue, which was found in a couple of our MITA Journeys, concerns information technology. Teachers were encouraged to share their weekly lesson plans with TAs so that they could review them ahead of time. However, audits revealed considerable variation in TAs' ability to access email or use cloud-based systems, such as Google Drive. In one school we worked with several years ago, we found that TAs had never been trained in how to use the staff email system. Imagine how many unopened emails with lesson plans attached were then found once the TAs were shown how to log in to their inboxes!

If our experience is anything to go by, it is likely that your staff audit will reveal a call from TAs to have a greater involvement in lesson planning. It is worth noting here that you may need to unpick *exactly* what TAs mean by this. For example, it could be an indication that there is not enough time to go through plans ahead of lessons with teachers, or to feedback afterwards. And/or it might suggest that they feel they do not have a sufficient level of involvement in planning, and what they are calling for is the chance to have a say in that process.

When it comes to TAs' day-to-day preparedness, we typically find that the audit reveals:

1   How much time, if any, teachers and TAs have to meet
2   If they have meeting time, how effectively it is used to brief TAs on lessons and receive quality feedback
3   If they do not have time to meet, how teachers communicate to TAs their lesson plans (i.e. tasks, activities, expected learning outcomes, and the TA's role in the lesson).

If teachers and TAs in your school do not have timetabled sessions in which to meet (i.e. within TAs' paid hours of work), you must change something to make such meetings part of the routine pattern of teacher–TA collaboration. We know from the DISS project that TAs worked, on average, an additional three hours voluntarily each week, spending much of that time in discussion with teachers. Many headteachers we interviewed were aware of how this could be seen as exploitative, though few had sought to do anything about it. They awkwardly admitted relying quite heavily on TAs' goodwill, as without it, there would likely be no teacher–TA liaison at all.

Many school leaders and teachers we have spoken to maintain that in order to get best value from their TAs, they should spend every working moment with pupils. There is a sound logic to this, of course, but there is also a strong case for using part of the TAs' time each week for planning and preparation, so they can be more effective the rest of the time when they are with pupils. If, for example, TAs lead interventions, consider the added value that would be derived from providing dedicated time for them to plan and prepare thoroughly for these sessions. We will look at this in detail in the following chapter, but our mantra regarding the use of interventions is that they should *at least* compensate for time pupils spend away from the teacher. But this cannot happen by solely putting your faith in the quality of the intervention programme. If you withdraw pupils from lessons for interventions, make the effort to ensure TAs have opportunities to properly prepare for their delivery, else you are unlikely to see the accelerated progress these programmes promise.

Creating the kind of time we are referring to is most effectively achieved by extending TAs' hours of work, and that of course costs money. In our developmental work with schools, we have been keen to emphasise and work towards creative solutions using existing resources; for example, using spaces in the school day in which teachers and TAs can meet, such as during teachers' PPA time or assemblies (see MITA Journeys box).

Changing TAs' hours of work does not necessarily mean you need to increase them. One possibility that emerged from the EDTA project was to retain the same number of contracted hours, but to shift start and end times, allowing teachers to have a set time for meeting with TAs, at the start or end of the school day. For example, one primary school brought the start and finish times of the TAs' days forward by 15 minutes. Implementing this, however, took about a year, as all of the TAs had slightly different start times. The leadership consulted and agreed with TAs on standardising a new start time, which was introduced at the start of the next school year. Though it took time to set up, this arrangement is now an established and effective practice.

It is worth noting that schools (albeit a minority) who have undertaken the MITA programme do make the investment in creating meeting time for TAs and teachers. In many cases, this recognises and formalises the kind of loose arrangement we mentioned above, often dating back years, that relies on TAs' goodwill. TAs at Crestwood were paid for the additional 15 minutes at the beginning of the day, before school, that they were coming in to meet with class teachers. One teacher described this change as 'probably one of the biggest changes to the organisation of the TAs', and vital in terms of acknowledging their commitment and contribution. At Laureate, a 'flexitime' arrangement was introduced, whereby each teacher–TA team arranges their own weekly meeting, and then the TA takes that time off in lieu at a convenient point in the week. As one teacher described it: 'We're very lucky that our TAs will come in early and stay late, but we recognise that they're doing that over and above. They deserve that time back.'

Whether you increase TAs' hours or rearrange them, ensuring that you do not trade excessively on TAs' goodwill sends a strong signal in terms of how you value them, as well as demonstrating your seriousness about ensuring they are fully prepared for their role. Furthermore, as we describe later, this recognition is frequently converted into impact.

MITA Journeys

'Maggie is taking assembly'

Using school assemblies to free up time for teachers and TAs to meet is a common response to the issue of a lack of liaison time. The MITA Journeys schools used this as part of their strategy to improve TAs' day-to-day preparedness. Scott, Headteacher at Cuddington Croft, explains how they did it at his school:

> We organised a timetable, so we [senior leaders] took on extra responsibility to run assembly. We made it a longer one, moving our celebration assembly from Fridays to Mondays, and stuck in another assembly on Friday. So Alice [Deputy Headteacher] and I will do celebration assembly, which tends to be the longest one of the week. You can be looking at 25 minutes for teachers and TAs to meet.

At Crestwood, the Headteacher, Maggie Stowe, took on the responsibility for leading the Monday morning assembly by herself, which meant all teachers and TAs could meet at the start of the week. A sign of how the staff valued this arrangement was how this weekly fixture became known as 'MITA time', where MITA was repurposed to stand for 'Maggie Is Taking Assembly'!

Here is how a teacher at Crestwood and a TA at Cuddington Croft (respectively) described the use of assembly for liaison time:

> We have a designated time on a Monday morning which is brilliant, because you get a chance to talk about what you planned. That's the opportunity... to talk about it with my TA and say, 'we could do it like this'. We're all sharing the planning and the ideas, and it's really, really helpful.
>
> It's great because it's at the beginning of the week and you have a clear idea as to what the plan is for each day, and there's an opportunity, a forum, to discuss, clarify, query anything. There was nothing like this before, and I find it invaluable.

It is important for you and your SLT to actively monitor the use of any liaison time you create. Simply providing space in the school day does not guarantee that teachers or TAs will know how to make best use of it. At the outset, you should make your expectations known about how the time should be used, and ensure you monitor what is going on by making regular checks. Be clear how preparation time should be used, and if necessary set out your expectations and provide examples. Everything should point back to how the use of liaison time will contribute to raising pupil attainment.

Protecting liaison time is important too. In one school we worked with, SLT were so keen that teachers and TAs use the 40 minutes at the end of the school day that had been costed and provided for joint planning and discussion, that they notified parents that teachers would not be available until these meetings were concluded at 4pm. While there were some sensible exceptions to this rule (e.g. an urgent safeguarding matter), it ensured that teachers and TAs could make a prompt start to their after-school preparation time, and make full use of it with minimal distraction.

Lesson planning

Teachers' overview of the curriculum, each unit of work, and the sequential development of concepts and understanding, all contribute to the formulation of a lesson plan. TAs tend not to have the same level of pedagogical awareness of the context in which any lesson plan can be set. Furthermore, the same TA may not be present lesson-to-lesson. All of this underscores the need to ensure that teachers' intentions are explicit. Teachers should not assume that writing the TA's initials against certain sections of the lesson plan is sufficient for communicating important information about learning expectations.

The need for the TA to guess what is in the teacher's mind must be reduced as far as possible. Just because teachers and leaders trust and respect TAs, we should not assume that they have the implicit knowledge teachers hold as the skilled pedagogues. Teachers need to provide TAs with detailed and clear information about the tasks they assign to them: key concepts, facts and information to be taught; skills to be learned, applied, practised or extended; and the intended outcomes, in terms of learning and tangible outputs. Think in terms of the lesson 'need to knows': the four or five critical things the TA will need to be aware of in order to make the best contribution to the lesson.

One way of formalising what you expect teachers to provide in terms of preparation for TAs is to develop a key information template: a framework that prompts teachers to think through and record what they need TAs to do during a lesson, and what they need to know in order to do it effectively and consistently. MITA Journeys schools, for example, used the teacher–TA agreement described in Chapter 5 as a way to structure lesson plans.

Some tasks teachers deploy TAs to undertake may be less pedagogical in nature than others, but should be made clear nonetheless in their planning. For example, teachers in early years settings commonly use TAs to observe and record pupil performance or engagement for assessment purposes during lessons. This is a smart way to use TAs, as observation requires identifying and recording responses to interactions, and does not require any intervention. TAs, however, must be trained to conduct observations reliably. TAs and early years support workers provide valuable data for teachers they might otherwise miss in a busy classroom of 30 or more young children. This information is used to compile each pupil's learning journey and feeds into teachers' further task planning and assessment. If you work in a school with an early years setting, there is much to be learned about TA preparation and deployment in this phase that can be imported into classrooms further up the school.

We are really clear that creating time for teachers and TAs to meet to plan and prepare lessons is the ideal situation. However, we should recognise that in some cases this just might not be possible. So, what can teachers do in this scenario? How can they make the most of the short moments they have with TAs? Firstly, ensure teachers make key information available to TAs as far in advance as possible. Sharing information early allows TAs to get back to teachers with any queries. This information is not only the primary mechanism for communicating lesson aims, but also the shared basis on which teachers and TAs can have conversations – even if (as is often the case) this is briefly at the start of the lesson. Where TAs receive information in advance, they are able to work through what they do and do not understand. This way, conversations are limited to clarifying anything the TA is unclear about, rather than running through, from the top, things they already know.

Secondly, changes to lesson plans are inevitable at times, and this is to be encouraged as good teachers deviate from their plan when they realise it is not working or when they recognise a better strategy is required. Teachers should ensure they alert TAs to any changes to their original plan if, for example, assessments from the previous lesson suggest a different approach is needed in the following lesson than that already shared with the TA. Such tweaks will be easier to convey once TAs have an awareness of the overall aim and content of the lesson. The situation to avoid is TAs finding themselves persisting with a particular strategy the teacher has rejected in favour of something more appropriate. This is not an uncommon experience for many TAs who do not see plans prior to lessons.

When TAs cover classes

Our research has shown the quality of information sharing prior to lessons is a key factor in whether lessons covered by TAs and cover supervisors run smoothly and pupils achieve. In the DISS project, we found that teachers avoided planning demanding lessons for planned absences – which is somewhat understandable given the expertise required to deliver them – and instead supplied pupils with 'busy work'.

But under-stimulating work increased the incidence of off-task and disruptive behaviour, which was in any event a challenge for TAs to deal with because the pupils were very aware the person in charge was someone they perceived to have less authority than a teacher. For teachers, the irony is that time saved by not planning for absence properly can be lost by having to follow up behaviour incidents on their return to school.

To protect TAs and cover supervisors, and to ensure as far as possible good classroom work and behaviour in teachers' absence, school leaders must address preparation for lesson cover and build it into the school's policies. TAs and cover supervisors should not be sold short by inadequately planned lessons. You will need to decide the appropriate lesson format and tasks teachers should be required to provide for TAs for planned absences. Teachers should ensure that information is annotated with specific instructions, or even thought of afresh with the TA in mind. They should ensure the covering TA is aware of where to find resources. If it is possible for teachers to know in advance which TA will be taking their lesson, encourage them to seek them out and brief them on the lesson plan. A member of SLT should monitor these processes as assiduously as they do for supply cover.

Key recommendations on the day-to-day preparedness of TAs

- Schools should make whatever adjustments are possible to suit the implementation of effective models of preparation, including adjusting TAs' existing working hours and/or contracts.
- Look for creative ways to timetable periods in the school day for teacher–TA liaison.
- Formalise the way teachers plan and share information about lessons by instituting a school-wide information sharing template and process for communication.
- Ensure teachers provide TAs with 'need to know' information for each lesson: be clear about the role TAs are to take; which pupils to support; what tasks to support; and what the expected outcomes are. Share information prior to lessons, and use time before lessons to discuss amendments.
- Set standards for what teachers must do to ensure TAs are properly prepared to cover lessons in their absence. Have clear expectations of what lesson plans must include.

Obtaining quality feedback from TAs using process success criteria

As we have noted at points throughout this book, TAs have a privileged position within the classroom. They are present at the moment learning happens. That said, learning is not something we can see directly, but we *can* observe its effects in the form of pupils' performance; that is, in the things they say and the work they produce. It is this detailed information on pupils' performance that teachers need in order to inform their planning and teaching. Quality feedback from TAs on how pupils engage with and perform tasks fuels future lesson planning, and completes the preparation loop. Although quick and easy, writing 'TA supported' in the page margin of an exercise book is unlikely to tell the teacher much about the type of support given.

Teachers need relevant and pointed feedback, and TAs require a clear sense of what this constitutes, else their interactions with pupils and any feedback they provide is likely to centre on task completion. Our sister publication, *The Teaching Assistants Guide to Effective Interaction*, sets out a role for TAs as collectors of accurate and detailed feedback *of* learning for the teacher to use in assessment *for* learning. Feedback is linked to the layers of the scaffolding framework (see Chapter 6) and focuses attention on the extent to which pupils are able to undertake the sequential steps of a task independently, and the type and amount of scaffolding they require. The approach we encourage is based on using process success criteria to structure feedback.

Process success criteria are all the steps or elements required to complete the overall task goal (the product) successfully. Each step is a 'mini-goal'. In order to scaffold effectively, TAs must be clear about each mini-goal, so that they can assess how much the pupil is able to do in relation to each one. Feedback set against process success criteria is far more useful to teachers than information about whether pupils completed a task, as it allows crucial steps in the learning journey to be recorded.

As we highlighted in Chapter 6, TAs in MITA Journeys schools used the scaffolding framework as the basis for feedback to teachers on pupils' performance. The requirement for teachers to think in terms of planning tasks for pupils with process success criteria (i.e. what can they do?), not product success criteria (i.e. what have they done?) in mind, was often described as a minor, but powerful change, to practice. As one teacher at Cuddington Croft put it: 'You're still planning as you normally do, but you're just changing the way you're thinking about your planning. It's a small tweak.' On a visit to the school, the teacher showed us how symbols linked to the scaffolding framework entered into a pupil's workbook by the TA, help to inform her planning and assessment. For the purposes of illustration, we shall call the pupil Max.

> Here, for example, I can see that the TA has assisted Max in more detail [by providing clues], because it's quite challenging. But here, she's supported for the first three steps, and then the last two, Max has done independently. Even with the extension tasks, by supporting rather than doing the whole thing, Max has done three steps through support and then been able to do the last two independently. It really helps with my assessment. My TA will write me notes or write down observations: 'I know that the work is independent'; or 'I think you need to reinforce this'. So, for the next lesson, before they move onto the next skill, I know who will need an opportunity to consolidate the day before, or if I need to have a focus group on that. It really does help with that.

You can find more information about using process success criteria to provide feedback, and how this relates to the scaffolding framework, in *The Teaching Assistants Guide*. Key recommendations on obtaining quality feedback from TAs

- Capitalise on the unique position TAs have in classrooms to capture detailed information on how pupils engage with and perform tasks, in order to inform future lesson planning.
- Consider structuring both the TA's role in the lesson and their feedback to teachers using process success criteria.

Summary

Earlier we made the point that your audit of current practice is likely to bring to light how TAs want to have a greater involvement in lesson planning, and how greater involvement usually means not just time to liaise with teachers, but to make a meaningful contribution to lessons. This can be sensitive territory to navigate, because not all teachers will want a TA's input into their planning. Some may consider this too great an encroachment on their professional turf. Others might feel that while it is desirable, it is logistically difficult to organise; for example, if a teacher prefers to plan lessons at home, it is impractical to involve the TA. We are not saying that TAs have a right to contribute to teachers' lesson planning, but where they are not, we believe that TAs have a right to be sufficiently appraised of what teachers expect from them in the classroom, and to know that they are suitably equipped to acquit themselves in line with those expectations. This is the essence of what we call preparedness.

In the case of the MITA Journeys schools, many of them drew TAs into the lesson planning process, with the effect of improving their confidence and how valued they were in the opinion of teachers. When we spoke to school leaders, TAs and teachers at these schools in preparation for this book, the word we heard over and over was 'teamwork'. The comments below, first from a TA from Crestwood and then a teacher from Cuddington Croft, are indicative of the kinds of changes to preparedness that occurred as a result of participating in the MITA programme. Both comments draw attention to how more collaborative and inclusive approaches have become standard practice.

> I just feel more confident that we know what we're doing. It's much better, because the planning is there. You know what you're doing at the beginning of the week and what you're leading up to. Previously, when we didn't have that, you were sort of like blind really; going into the lessons, thinking 'what are we doing?'
>
> Where the teachers and TAs are working together... our TAs feel that they have been able to share ideas. So, they'll say to us, 'we know this works really well, but if we've got SATs coming up, for example, could we try this? I think this would really benefit the children'. So, they're having their voice heard, and we put that lesson in place or we've made those adaptations... Planning as a collaborative team; everybody's together as a team. I think that's really built in over the last two years.

Note

1 In the iterations of the survey before this (2014 and 2015), researchers used a less nuanced scale, and although NQTs rated their preparation to deploy TAs higher (67 per cent for both years), preparation for this aspect of teaching was still lower relative to other aspects (NCTL 2015).

Chapter 8

Maximising the impact of structured interventions delivered by TAs

Introduction

Although our MITA programme centres predominantly on the role of TAs inside classrooms, this book would be incomplete without sharing what we know about the deployment of TAs to deliver 'off-the-shelf' structured interventions and catch-up programmes.[1] To reiterate a key point from our review of the research in Chapter 1, the best evidence we have of the impact of TAs on learning is in relation to the delivery of such programmes. The international evidence is stacking up behind TA-led one-on-one and small group instruction in literacy and numeracy in a remarkably consistent fashion (Alborz et al. 2009; Sharples 2016; Slavin 2016, Nickow, Oreopoulos and Quan 2020). Evidence alone from a dozen trials of TA-led interventions funded by the EEF, from the early years to Year 7, shows that pupils can make, on average, two to three months additional progress, compared to those in a control condition.

It is easy to get seduced by the results of evaluations, trials and impact assessments – especially when school leaders are presented with data on widening gaps in progress among groups of pupils. It is not just the strength of the evidence that adds to the appeal of TA-led interventions, it is its cost-effectiveness too. In many respects, this model of TA deployment is the best embodiment of our MITA maxim: supplement, not replace, the teacher.

Yet what also emerges strongly from this evidence base is that pupils *only* make progress when TAs have been properly trained to deliver programmes. So, the main issue is not *whether* schools should deploy TAs to deliver interventions (the answer to that is an emphatic 'yes'!), it is *how* to do it so that the chances of obtaining the kind of impact reported in formal evaluations are fully optimised. This returns us again to a key theme of this book: implementation.

In this chapter, we will consider how to maximise the impact of teaching assistants in the context of structured interventions, by exploring and expanding on recommendations 5, 6 and 7 of the EEF guidance report, which we introduced in Chapter 1 (see Box 1.1).

Assessing claims about intervention impact

The SEND Code of Practice emphasises the use of evidence-based approaches to raising pupil attainment. This principle also applies to pupils who are not identified as having SEND, but are falling behind their peers in terms of age-related expectations. It is essential that where interventions are deployed as part of your SEND or catch-up provision, you adopt well-structured programmes with reliable evidence of effectiveness. Before we discuss how to go about achieving this, it is worth providing a quick crash course in how to read the results of evaluations of such programmes, and how to assess the claims made about interventions.

Not all assessments of interventions are equal, and a little research literacy is required in order to sift promising programmes from overhyped opportunities. Imagine you have received an unsolicited marketing email from an education company regarding a particular programme that claims a miraculous 12 months of progress in reading in just three months of delivery. If it sounds too good to be true, it probably is. Spend some time looking for and unpicking the claim and the evidence on which it is based. Here are a few questions to ask yourself about the claims being made:

- How many pupils or schools were involved in the evaluation? The lower the tally, the more sceptical you should be.
- How was impact measured, and what data and instruments were used? This should always be conveyed in terms school leaders and teachers can intuitively understand.
- Who conducted the evaluation? Was it carried out by a reliable independent third party, or was it an in-house job?
- Could other factors explain the impact reported? Remember: correlation does not mean causation. Any independent evaluation worth its salt will consider external factors.

Incidentally, the lack of availability of data to support a claim about an intervention is another warning sign. If you are unable to find information from a trustworthy source – for example, the University of York's Evidence 4 Impact or the EEF – do not waste any more of your time; stop and look at alternative options.

Here are a few more general points to consider about interventions. Firstly, some evaluations measure impact on pupil progress *in relation to* the intervention programme itself. Most off-the-shelf packages come with a tool to take baseline and progress measures, but these relate to the content and coverage of the programme. They can give you a progress score, but it might not be relatable to wider, more familiar forms of measurement and assessment associated with a particular subject. Secondly, be mindful about extrapolating effects. Results from a specific programme delivered to pupils in a specific year group (possibly in specific schools in a specific area) are unable to tell us much about progress outside of these parameters. In other words, the intervention might be successful for some pupils under certain conditions, but not others.

Finally, there is the effect of what is called 'fidelity to the programme'. This describes how faithful delivery of the programme is to its protocols and instructions. Some element of internal assessment is necessary and normal for a new intervention as it is readied for market. While finding some proof of impact can, of course, be helpful, the main purpose of this initial development process is to stress-test the programme, to find any flaws, and to identify where refinements are needed. Through the process of early small-scale piloting and testing, programme developers will arrive at a set of well-specified protocols and instructions, which in turn provide the kind of consistency and confidence that is the basis for a robust, reliable, ideally large-scale, and independently-evaluated trial. Be alive to issues of fidelity when reviewing the evidence on and claims made about a particular programme. If it is unclear whether the schools involved delivered the programme in the way the developers intended, there is a reasonable chance the results may have been influenced by undocumented factors. If changes are made to any part of the programme, the programme itself changes, and with it the chances of its success.

Reviewing programmes and processes

TA-led interventions are commonly delivered in one-to-one and small group contexts, away from the classroom. Despite compelling evidence of their impact, this must not lead to a situation where we pile the responsibility for pupils making accelerated progress onto TAs. As we have noted already, the SEND Code of Practice makes it clear that it is teachers who are responsible and accountable for pupil progress. Furthermore, interventions, however impactful, should not be used as a substitute for quality-first teaching.

If you are going to take pupils out of lessons for a TA-led programme, it should *at least* compensate for the time spent away from the teacher. This straightforward prerequisite should guide your planning and delivery. It also draws attention to two factors regarding interventions, over and above TAs, that school leaders ought to consider. These are: (i) thinking about the content and coverage of interventions themselves; and (ii) *who* is best placed to deliver them to particular groups of pupils.

Let us start with the second point. Although not many studies ask whether the impact would have been greater if the programme had been delivered by a teacher, rather than a TA, there is evidence to show that experienced and specifically trained teachers get the better results (Higgins et al. 2013; Slavin et al. 2009; Slavin 2016, Nickow, Oreopoulos and Quan 2020). It is important to take into consideration the extent of learning gaps when planning interventions, and to ask yourself whether there is a case for the teacher to lead the intervention, or to at least deliver some of the sessions. It is worth holding in mind that there is evidence (although, again, not extensive) indicating that TAs outperform volunteers when they deliver interventions. It is essential that you think about *which* staff teach *which* pupils and *which* groups, else you are at risk of widening gaps rather than closing them. If your furthest-behind pupils are steadily making progress, but their peers are making even more through teacher-led teaching back in the classroom, the gap will grow even as you try to close it. In short, it pays to disrupt the convention that TAs are the default setting when it comes to running interventions.

A strong determinant of success with any intervention is, not surprisingly, the quality of its content and coverage. So, the second factor school leaders need to consider is the programme materials. TAs are unlikely to outperform the incoherent design, poor resources, or incomplete instructions that characterise weak programmes. Here, then, we recommend carrying out an 'interventions health check'. This will help you to identify any programmes that are ineffective, and would be ineffective regardless of who delivered them. Below, we have listed some questions to ask:

An interventions health check

- Do we select interventions that have a sound evidence base demonstrating success?
- If so, are they being used as intended, with the appropriate guidance and training? Or do we use good programmes badly?
- What are the aims and objectives of each of our intervention programmes?
- How does this cohere with the aims, objectives and coverage of our wider curriculum?
- How do we evaluate pupil progress and the effectiveness of interventions?

- What do our data show for pupils involved in interventions? Is it in line with the expected progress from the research and/or suggested by the programme developer?
- Do we ever adjust or even close down any ineffective programmes?

In addition, a health check can support the process of agreeing a clear and shared definition of what counts as an intervention. We mention this because we have heard of schools using this term to describe homespun programmes that are loosely structured and poorly targeted.

Common features of effective interventions

As we have discussed, the evidence on TA-led interventions is maturing well, and from it we are beginning to get a stronger handle on the common features of what makes for an effective and impactful programme. What we are learning draws together elements of intervention design (i.e. the materials and resources) and implementation (i.e. how it is rolled out and integrated with the wider curriculum offer and the delivery of mainstream teaching). Here is an overview of commonly occurring features found among effective interventions.

Firstly, there is length and duration. Effective programmes are composed of brief sessions (ranging 20–50 minutes), timetabled to run regularly (3–5 times per week), and maintained over a sustained period (8–20 weeks). Secondly, the amount and type of training, coaching and support provided by the school for staff delivering interventions makes a critical difference to the effectiveness and impact. Effective programmes ensure TAs receive extensive training from experienced trainers and/or teachers (5–30 hours per intervention).[2] Thirdly, the materials are of a high quality. The intervention has structured supporting resources and lesson plans, with clear objectives and possibly a delivery script.

The fourth feature is fidelity, the significance of which we mentioned above. This is an easy one to overlook, and schools can often fall into the 'fidelity trap'. Consider this: you are persuaded that your school should invest in an intervention designed to improve vocabulary skills for children in the early years. Results from a large-scale, robust and independently-evaluated randomised trial found that pupils who received the intervention made up to four months of additional progress, compared to pupils in the control condition. You read that the programme should be delivered over a 15-week period to small groups of no more than four pupils, three times a week, for 20 minutes at a time. These were the conditions under which the evaluation was conducted and found successful. To stand a chance of achieving similar outcomes, it is imperative not to deviate from the delivery protocols. You may have an above-average number of children in your setting who urgently need this intervention, but avoid tinkering with these essential variables. Rather than run it with groups of six pupils, or have back-to-back 40-minute sessions, run more sessions with appropriately-sized groups.

Finally, there is one more crucial fidelity factor: sticking to the script. If a programme has a script to aid delivery, ensure TAs adhere to it. Likewise, ensure TAs closely follow the plan and structure of the intervention overall and for each session. These materials may be adaptable for future cohorts, but not before TAs know them inside-out and can use them faithfully.

Implementation matters

As we have made clear, the central question about TA-led interventions is less an issue of 'what works' and more a matter of 'how to make them work'. We complete this chapter by discussing several additional aspects of implementation that are essential for capitalising on the potential of promising programmes.

Intervention specialists

The fidelity issues we have just outlined give rise to a question of whether it is worth deploying TAs as 'intervention specialists'. In an average-sized, two-form entry primary school, for example, having one or two TAs fully dedicated to the delivery of curriculum catch-up programmes may have strategic value. Consider some of the advantages. The role may suit and optimise the knowledge and skills of TAs with a background or degree-level qualification in a literacy or numeracy-related subject, and thereby provide them with a clear purpose and professional identity (see Chapter 6). Specialists would become experts in a small number of carefully selected programmes; practice is less diffuse, and greater consistency and quality in delivery is ensured. Training is easier and cheaper to organise, especially if it is delivered off-site. Teachers would have a single point of contact for planning and discussing pupil progress.

We have seen a similar model used in a few secondary schools. The responsibility of managing intervention programmes was relocated from the SEND Support unit to the English and Maths departments. Subject teachers were given the responsibility for coordinating the day-to-day roles of TAs. Centralising 'catch-up' ensured teachers had full control of the factors they needed to plan effective provision. It resulted in greater integration of the intervention coverage into the wider curriculum, and planning, preparation and feedback between teachers and the specialist TA was easier to coordinate, and arrived in a timelier fashion.

The involvement of teachers

While interventions can be delivered by TAs, it is important that this does not drift towards them assuming responsibility. As the secondary school example above implies, the greater the involvement of teachers, the more likely you are to capitalise on TA-led interventions.

The DISS project called attention to the widespread lack of teacher involvement with, and general ignorance of, the content, teaching and outcomes of TA-led programmes. The purpose of any intervention is to produce a payoff in terms of improving overall end-of-year attainment in an area of weakness (e.g. reading). A surer route to achieving this is the greater involvement of teachers in the preparation and delivery of interventions. It is important that where TAs deliver interventions, teachers do not become detached from the broad aims and effectiveness of the programmes used and the specific content and objectives of individual sessions. Given that teachers are responsible for learning outcomes, they need to have a stake in:

- The selection, preparation and assessment of interventions.
- Decisions about where and when TAs deliver the programmes. If pupils need to be withdrawn from lessons, which lessons will they be withdrawn from?

- Ensuring the quality and effectiveness of teaching approaches used by TAs.
- Possible involvement in the delivery of interventions.
- Establishing a process of specific and (at least) weekly feedback from TAs on pupil performance.
- Integrating, extending, relating and consolidating the learning gained from intervention sessions in whole-class input and work with individuals and groups.

That last point is crucial, as you can get an extra shot of impact on progress when teachers and TAs bridge learning by making explicit connections between out-of-class interventions and teaching back in the classroom. Too often it can be left to pupils to make such links. This bridging is all the more essential given that these are the pupils who find accessing and applying learning difficult in the first place. A simple example: if the morning intervention group has been working on a particular phonics blend, ensure teachers and TAs look for opportunities for pupils to practise applying that blend in the classroom throughout the day. Teachers could also ask pupils to show them where they have used new learning from the most recent intervention session in their writing.

While we have been discussing interventions in implicit terms as being delivered outside the classroom, teachers could explore the prospect of delivering an intervention session inside the classroom, while the TA roves the class (see Chapter 5). We have found in cases where teachers and TAs have received the same training in a particular programme, there is a greater integration of the learning achieved by pupils in the intervention sessions with their wider classroom experience.

Either way, the key is for teachers to view the intervention from the pupils' point of view and ensure they enrich their learning experiences, building on and making relevant the time spent out of class. When teachers have greater awareness of pupils' learning from interventions, they can draw those concepts, facts, skills and understanding developed in the withdrawal sessions into their lesson planning, and, when pupils return to lessons, ask questions that help them apply, demonstrate and consolidate new learning.

The integration of specific programmes with the mainstream curriculum, together with the alignment with pupils' curriculum targets, is vital to building on the positive gains that research has shown can be obtained by deploying TAs to deliver quality interventions.

Targeting and matching

Effective interventions ensure the right support is being provided to the right child at the right time. This is why it is no good trying to match pupils to interventions that are past their best. The reason why this happens is quite understandable: training is expensive; TAs are often time poor; you need pupils to catch up quickly. It is easier to work with what you have, however imperfect, than start again with a new programme and additional training demands. But the evidence clearly points to impact stemming from well-targeted interventions, delivered by well-trained TAs. Remember: a minimum expectation is that out-of-class interventions should at least compensate for time away from the class and the teacher. There is always a case for pragmatism and flexibility, but be mindful about what you are willing to compromise on.

There is a further issue concerning targeting and matching that is worth considering, and that is the potential to shape and reinforce peer groups. Be aware that when a child is withdrawn from the class for an intervention, the peer support group you relocate them to may be less effective than the one you remove them from. Consider this: your school runs a programme for pupils with speech and language difficulties. The TA works heroically on developing their communication skills, but by design and definition, the one thing these pupils do not get from these sessions is good modelling of speech and language from their peers. Think about the composition of groups and how interventions could work differently for at least some of the time. This will allow you to make the most of peer supports and provide opportunities for struggling pupils to mix with a wider group of classmates, rather than always with each other.

Timetabling

Here is another reason why the involvement of teachers and leaders in planning interventions is so important. Several years ago, we had a large secondary school participate in the MITA programme. The auditing process revealed, much to the dismay of the headteacher, that pupils were being withdrawn from interventions to do interventions! This is rare, of course, but it is not uncommon for pupils in some settings to find themselves on a carousel of interventions.

Timetabling is, therefore, another crucial implementation factor. Carefully schedule sessions to enable consistent delivery, and minimise the amount of time pupils spend away from the class. While consistency matters, be mindful too of which lessons pupils are withdrawn from. We have seen, for example, that if you take a sports-mad child out of PE to do extra maths, they are unlikely to be in a state where they are receptive to learning. If this happens week after week, they may become resentful. It is not much fun for the TA either. Once again, the point to consider is whether the time spent in an intervention is sufficiently compensating for time away from mainstream lessons.

One final important element of timetabling is sticking to it. This may sound rather obvious, but we have seen for ourselves many times over that intervention sessions are easily hijacked. Shepherding children from all corners of the playground and ushering them into the building, collecting up left-behind jumpers and coats, or tending to a bleeding knee, these things eat into the start of the afternoon timetable for TAs who carry out lunch duty. If you schedule intervention sessions for directly after lunchtime, it is possible that they do not often start on time. Instead, build in some leeway time, and start the sessions 15 minutes later.

Here is another common scenario TAs have described to us. Jo (a TA) is on her way to collect her first group of the day for a reading intervention, when she is spotted by the deputy headteacher who hastily redeploys her to a Year 3 classroom to cover a staff absence. The clear power dynamic means that Jo cannot easily refuse, so she heads off to Year 3 for the morning. Result: the pupils in Jo's reading group miss out on their intervention session. Why does this matter? Well, consider the unintended message this sends to those children: 'Your reading really, really matters – but just not today'. These children can then lose out twice over. Not only do they miss their scheduled intervention slot, but elements of the lesson from which they would have been withdrawn may be less accessible, because the teacher, not unreasonably, planned it on the basis of those pupils not being present. Coverage and tasks are therefore insufficiently differentiated, and in a further complication, there is no TA to provide support. Do not underestimate the knock-on effect that this could have on a child's motivation and their appetite for interventions.

Timetabling inconsistencies can also leave TAs like Jo with the impression that their hard work on delivering interventions is not valued. This is another reason why appointing some intervention specialists (see above) and a TA dedicated lesson cover (see Chapter 5) could be useful.

Summary

In this chapter, we have considered how to review the programmes and processes of curriculum interventions, and how to optimise the role and impact of TAs in their delivery. There are a number of factors that school leaders need to consider in relation to TA-led interventions, but the evidence suggests that spending time and effort on refining a catch-up strategy could be well rewarded. We conclude this chapter by briefly summarising some key recommendations.

Key recommendations on TA-led interventions

- Carry out a 'health check' of the interventions you use. Look for evidence to support the claims made about them, and be willing to ditch any interventions not producing benefits for pupils.
- Consider creating specialist roles for TAs around intervention delivery, and potentially increasing the involvement of teachers in delivery, especially if pupils' needs and learning gaps demand it.
- As well as delivery, encourage teachers to have a greater stake and involvement in the selection, preparation and assessment of interventions. Ensure teachers are informed about the programmes used, and that the selection of a specific programme aligns with pupils' individual needs and their curriculum targets.
- Be mindful of when interventions are timetabled and whether groups could be composed differently for at least some sessions in order to capitalise on peer learning and modelling.

Notes

1 In this book, we define structured interventions programmes as highly structured courses of input designed to supplement classroom teaching and achieve specific leaning outcomes. These, what we might call, 'off-the-shelf', 'oven-ready' programmes are typically commercially available. To be clear, we exclude from our definition any 'homemade' programmes that have been put together by a teacher or SENCO, and are unique to a particular setting.
2 School-based programmes set by allied health professionals (e.g. an occupational therapist or a speech and language therapist), but in the main delivered by TAs, can provide a good model for oversight and review. Typically, the specialist shares a programme tailored to the needs of the pupil, leads a shared session with the TA, then observes a TA-led session at an interim session to monitor fidelity, before joining the final session to evaluate and assess progress.

Chapter 9

Conclusions

In this final chapter, we draw together some key messages and general conclusions from the MITA Journeys schools about implementing the MITA process. We also share some indications of impact, based on our extensive work on supporting schools to improve the deployment, practice and preparedness of their TAs, and discuss their implications in the context of the 'what works' agenda.

Acting on the evidence

Much of the evidence on effective use of TAs can be summarised in one clear principle: deploy TAs to supplement what teachers do, not replace them. You will recognise this as the second of the seven recommendations taken from the EEF guidance report, *Making Best Use of Teaching Assistants*, which we outlined in Chapter 1, and around which we quite intentionally came to reframe and re-present MITA a couple of years after it launched. If you review the remaining recommendations, you will notice that they are either an exemplification of this core principle (e.g. the careful deployment of TAs to deliver structured interventions) or a way of achieving it (e.g. ensuring TAs are prepared for their roles). You will also notice how the wider pedagogical role model, which emerged from the DISS project, provides the empirical ballast.

We often talk about the recommendations in the EEF report as providing a basecamp: a secure pitch from which school leaders can set out on their MITA Journey. As with a previous iteration of this title, we have used this book to flesh out a more expansive version of the EEF guidance, which provides additional information and evidence to help school leaders map a course and navigate it successfully. The individuality of your course will be defined by your context (e.g. your setting, staff and pupil cohorts). This flexibility is deliberate and essential, because there is no one-size-fits-all solution to optimising the role and contribution of TAs.

As we set out in the early part of this book, the evidence is relatively straightforward, and there are strong indications that there are clear benefits to be had from addressing the way TAs are used, in terms of pupil outcomes, school outcomes and overall staff satisfaction and morale. All that said, our experiences of working with schools in improving the way TAs are deployed and prepared suggests that making those changes is less straightforward. This, of course, is why this book has such a relentless focus on the processes of implementation, which again we have based on an intuitive theory developed by John Kotter on bringing about and embedding lasting and transformative organisational change.

Putting MITA into action can be a complex process, requiring changes across all layers of the school – from the senior leadership downwards – that confront existing and inefficient ways of working, training at all levels, and oftentimes, structural changes relating to timetabling and contractual arrangements. Encouragingly, though, we know that schools that have overcome practical barriers to change frequently did so by investing time, attention and effort into making improvements. So, here is the good news: change on the scale we are advocating does not require you to spend lots of money. Furthermore, most of the schools we hear from that undertake MITA, including our MITA Journeys schools, report that impact often stems from the accrual of marginal gains, rather than as a result of wholesale change.

Making MITA happen: four key themes

As you would expect, school leaders subscribe to the MITA programme in order to improve the way they deploy TAs, and there is, of course, much that they can learn about this. But when we work with cohorts of school leaders, we make time to collectively capture and distil what we sometimes call the 'meta-learning'. We do this at the agreed point, usually after two or three terms of collaboration, when the input from our team scales back and our role shifts to facilitating schools to learn from one other by sharing their journeys and practical strategies.

What we and school leaders always find interesting about these meta-learning conversations is how little they have to do with TAs. Instead, they centre on the wider processes of implementation, on school leadership, and the role and influence of school culture. We have conducted this meta-learning exercise many times over with hundreds of schools, and there are four key themes that regularly emerge. We outline them here, acknowledging how they resonate and align with the messages from MITA Journey schools we described in Chapter 3.

Theme 1. A shared vision

There is no substitute for taking the time to develop a clear, coherent, whole-school strategic vision for TA deployment. Having a well-defined view of where you, as a school leader, want to take your staff, and agreeing a shared language for talking about it, is critical for securing buy-in. To momentarily revisit our analogies of basecamps and maps, you want your staff to willingly join you on the journey; you do not want any of them to feel left behind or risk getting lost along the way. Consistent messaging and re-messaging can provide anchoring points to help orientation. For example, in Chapter 2 we discussed how defining 'support' can provide clarity about roles, and in Chapter 3 we saw how the leadership team at Alver Valley kept circling back to earlier steps of the change process in order to bring all staff on board.

Involving staff from the outset is key. Providing opportunities for the views of each and every stakeholder to be heard and respected creates and cements buy-in to your vision. So too can linking MITA to other school improvement aims. If, for example, reducing teachers' workload is a strategic priority for your school, look for the ways in which MITA can facilitate that aim.

Theme 2. Esteeming and professionalising the TA role

MITA schools find something particularly empowering and impactful about establishing clarity regarding the role and contribution of TAs. Taking the time, as part of the vision-setting process, to debate and capture the essentialness of TAs' role in *your* school and the unique contributions they make not only helps establish boundaries with the teachers' role, but draws to the surface the things that simply *would not happen* (as frequently, if at all) were it not for your TA workforce.

We began this book by inviting you to imagine your school without TAs, which no doubt revealed to you how integral they are. We find that when schools unpack and recognise what TAs do, their value becomes starkly apparent. We have, on occasion, heard school leaders admit to undervaluing the work TAs do, and they use this as motivation to strengthen their commitment to MITA and to invest in their TAs.

We have made a strong case for rethinking the role of your TAs in terms of supporting pupils to develop independence. Many MITA schools achieve this via our Maximising the Practice of Teaching Assistants (MPTA) training and/or by working through the book on which MPTA is based: *The Teaching Assistant's Guide to Effective Interaction*. Schools report that these efforts to improve TAs' practice give them a renewed sense of purpose; the clear and potentially transformative role they can have in improving pupils' independence is linked to feelings of empowerment, improved self-confidence, self-esteem and sense of 'actually owning something'. These sentiments were echoed by a number of teachers we spoke to as part of the MITA Journeys interviews (see also comments from school leaders in Chapter 3). This comment from a teacher from Shirley Manor was indicative of what we heard:

> I think it's made teaching assistants a lot more confident in their own practice, and made them have more ownership of what they're doing.

The concept of ownership is a relatively new discovery for us, and one that we think is potentially significant, as it talks to the issue of professional identity we discussed in Chapter 6. Allied to this is the tendency for this to express itself in the form of TAs engaging more often in professional conversations, which as a TA from Laureate put it, also helped to forge a collegiate spirit:

> MITA has brought us together, talking more. Absolutely. I think, as TAs, we have had a lot more conversations. I know we have. Even just in the staff room like: 'I'm not really sure about this' and 'I've noticed that'. We have chatted more. We've learned from each other.

Theme 3. Thinking through implementation

The third meta-learning theme is an explicit recognition of the significance of implementation. School leaders that take the wider view acknowledge that by underpinning the introduction of any new evidence-based approach – be it in relation to improving TA deployment, designing and rolling out a new curriculum, or some other school initiative – with change management processes enhances the whole endeavour and improves (though does not guarantee) the chances of success.

When we ask school leaders to identify the stages of the MITA approach that they felt were most helpful, what we find they actually do is cite the steps from Kotter's model: develop a clear, logical, well-specified aim and programme of work; form a development team to help with buy-in, build capacity and channel energy from any sceptical or resistance forces; specify tight areas amenable to change, which could lead to early wins; trial strategies on a small scale, win support and play the long game; and maintain the profile of what you are doing so that momentum does not drop.

Theme 4. Leadership and culture

A constant refrain in this book has been this: in order to bring about the necessary change, it is important that leadership comes from the headteacher. It is not enough, as some school leaders have assumed, to assign the job of reform to the SENCO or another member of staff, especially if they are not members of the SLT.

This conclusion about leadership is hardly unique. A raft of research attests to why head-teachers must drive, not dodge, school workforce issues. School leaders participating in the MITA programme have been driven by a desire to ensure TAs' contribution to school life seriously counts, *as well as* a need to understand why pupils targeted for TA support are adversely affected by the very intervention designed to help them, and how to reverse this situation.

Implicit in everything we have been saying in this book is the role of school leadership and its relationship to school culture. A strong and consistent message from headteachers has been that, while they may have begun their journey seeking to change the practice of TAs, the real challenge has been changing the mindsets of their teachers. That task is necessarily the responsibility of the headteacher, and so without strong leadership we are unlikely to move much beyond where we currently are. And that affects school culture. People become fatigued, resentful and complacent, and when that reaches a critical mass, toxicity levels rise and the culture, and indeed the workings, of the whole school can, in the worst cases, become dysfunctional and acrimonious.

If, as the popular aphorism from the business world goes, culture is 'the way we do things around here', then it was gratifying to hear that MITA Journeys schools were well on the way to naturalising the kinds of practices described in this book, and integrating them into *their* way of doing things. As a teacher at Cuddington Croft put it: 'It's now our practice. It's the way we are'.

To be clear, we are not saying that MITA can remedy deep cultural issues. However, we do think that the underpinning principles and processes of implementation and managing change on which MITA is built have a wider power and potential to positively impact school culture. This view was neatly summarised for us once by a primary school leader on a bright yellow post-it note that we collected during one of our meta-learning activities, and which we have reproduced below with the original underlining and capitalisation:

Impact because part of whole school culture NOT BOLT ON.

Indications of impact

The post-it note leads us to an important concluding question: what is the impact of Maximising the Impact of Teaching Assistants?

The outcomes of the Effective Deployment of Teaching Assistants (EDTA) project, which established the principles and processes for the MITA programme, found that schools made improvements to the ways in which teachers deployed and prepared TAs. Engaging in the project was professionally important for all staff. Teachers became more aware of their responsibilities to pupils and TAs, and it was clear the TAs felt more valued, appreciated, and more confident in their role and abilities (for more, see Webster, Russell and Blatchford 2016).

Early evaluations based on the first cohorts of schools to complete MITA in 2014/15, based on feedback from participants, found that despite starting from different points, all schools made progress towards understanding and addressing the complex issues of rethinking the TA role and raising the profile of TAs within their school. The effects these schools described broadly echo what we present below in terms of impact in the MITA Journeys schools.

With the development of the MPTA training and the publication of *The Teaching Assistant's Guide to Effective Interaction*, we have taken the work on TA–pupil interactions to a new level. Hundreds of UK schools have accessed MPTA in order to unlock the enormous potential of TAs to help *all* pupils develop the essential skills that underpin learning, such as the ability to scaffold their own learning and ask the questions that help them to get better at getting better at learning. Feedback from schools on MPTA is consistently positive, and (as we noted above) is routinely cited in relation to observable improvements in TAs' confidence and effectiveness in the classroom.

In this book, we have sought to build on these early signs of impact by drawing together what we have learned about maximising the impact of teaching assistants. Our approach to this has been to use a small set of intensive case studies, which are indicative of the real-world experiences of the many primary schools that have undertaken the MITA programme. By zeroing in on these schools, we can tell an authentic story about implementation and impact, which not only showcases their successes, but importantly, does not gloss over the realities and challenges schools typically face when they engage deeply and purposefully in this process. Indeed, it is through engaging with these realities and challenges that important lessons can be learned.

In Chapter 3, we described some encouraging indicators of impact as reported by senior leaders from our MITA Journeys schools. To this we can add evidence obtained from TAs and teachers in relation to (i) the MPTA training on scaffolding for independence, and (ii) teacher workload, all of which very much echo school leaders' views.

Practitioners reported that directly after the MPTA training, there was a noticeable improvement in the quality of TAs' practice. Specifically, that they left more wait time in their interactions with pupils, and were operating with the 'least help first' principle at the fore of their practice. Teachers had certainly noticed the changes to TAs' practice and the impact this had on pupils' independence:

> TAs are more confident in what they're doing on a one-to-one basis or in a group basis, and helped them to step back from spoon-feeding children – which a lot of them probably did previously. Now they're allowing the children do stuff on their own before they intervene.
>
> Shirley Manor

It has, I think, significantly helped our children, not just academically, but also in terms of their independence, their confidence, their ability to problem-solve, to be able to just get on, and their focus and concentration.

Cuddington Croft

The positive comments from teachers about TAs' practice were frequently linked to reflections they had about their workload. In our collaborations with schools, we are especially mindful to not imply that MITA will add to teachers' workload. In fact, we emphasise that by improving the deployment of TAs, and by ensuring that they can fulfil the roles they are given confidently and competently, teachers' workload can in fact be reduced. When we asked teachers in the MITA Journeys schools about the impact on their workload, their responses suggested a rebalancing had taken place:

I really don't think it has made a huge difference to our workload. I'd say it's made a tiny difference to my workload. And actually if that's going to impact the children and it's going to have a positive effect, then it's worth it.

Cuddington Croft

I think it has very much been a different workload instead of more workload. Swapping policy on marking and things like that, so that it's effective and not more, on top of.

Shirley Manor

I think it's given and it's taken away. Arming TAs with the knowledge of what you're doing increases their confidence in terms of doing the marking.

Laureate

[Because change was incremental] I don't think you really notice any extra work. I think you benefit in the long run as well. I think the benefits outweigh any extra effort that's put in in the beginning.

Crestwood

To reiterate our earlier point, we think it is encouraging that these comments speak to forms of impact that resulted from tweaks to practice, as opposed to a comprehensive overhaul.

Further indications and interpretations of impact

We know that when making decisions about which approaches to teaching and learning to adopt, schools are more influenced by what seems to work in other schools and the experiences of other teachers, than they are by academic research (Walker et al. 2019). The authentic and detailed accounts from MITA Journeys schools we have reported in this book provide valuable testimony to this effect. This evidence shows that when school leaders take seriously the empirical evidence on TA deployment, practice and preparation, and work hard with their TAs and teachers on making improvements, an array of positive impacts can follow. These reports echo numerous other personal testimonials we have heard from other school leaders, teachers and TAs that have undertaken MITA.

To find out whether MITA has an impact on pupils' academic progress, we ideally need to do an appropriately scaled, randomised trial. While this was not the focus of our MITA Journeys project, we have completed a roll-out of MITA that has been the focus of an independently evaluated efficacy trial, using a randomised controlled trial (RCT) design (see EEF 2017). This project, which concluded in 2019 and was funded by the EEF, involved over 120 primary schools in England. Thankfully, the delivery of the MITA programme and MPTA training to these schools, and the collection of data to measure its impact (including pupil attainment data), were all conducted and completed long before the disruption caused by the Covid-19 health emergency. However, the completion of the analyses by the independent evaluator (appointed by the EEF) incurred a delay due to the pandemic.

At the time of writing (Autumn 2020), the independent evaluation of the MITA RCT had not been completed. There is, however, evidence from other projects that were influenced by or very similar to MITA – and with which we have had some involvement – that shows impact in primary settings.

In Chapters 1 and 3, we cited evidence from independent evaluations of two large-scale campaigns in schools across Yorkshire and Lincolnshire, which had essentially the same purpose as MITA: to roll out the recommendations in the *Making Best Use of Teaching Assistants* guidance. Findings from an independent evaluation of the Yorkshire project, which involved nearly 1,000 primary schools, suggest we can be cautiously optimistic about its impact. Researchers found a mild positive impact on pupil attainment in English at Key Stage 2 (Sibieta and Sianesi 2019); equivalent to just under a month's additional progress.

Although both the EEF guidance and the coverage of these regional campaigns draw heavily on our approach, these evaluations do not amount to a verdict on the impact of MITA itself. They do, however, raise some important points that are relevant and relatable to MITA.

The first point is the nature and size of the main impact measure: pupil attainment. For anyone looking at the Yorkshire result and thinking that the amount of additional progress pupils made looks a little on the modest side, it is worth restating the general observation made elsewhere in this book that finding a positive impact on learning via a randomised trial operating at the scale of the Yorkshire campaign is really quite rare. More immediately, when it comes to research on the impact of TAs in everyday classrooms, let us not lose sight of the fact that the most rigorous study on this topic before this – the DISS project – found a negative relationship between TA support and pupil progress. Viewed this way, the departure point for our improvement journey is not a neutral starting line, but a position some yards *behind* it. What we see in the attainment results from the Yorkshire project suggests that the ineffective practices that best explained the DISS project results can not only be offset, but inverted.

The second point to make is, for us, perhaps the most crucial, because it talks to the specific types of impact that are the direct target of MITA. The principal aim of MITA is to improve schools' strategic decision-making and to equip them to challenge and change ineffective operational approaches, in order to create the kinds of conditions and processes that can *in turn* impact positively on pupils' learning outcomes. The evaluations of both Yorkshire and Lincolnshire projects found statistically significant changes to some of the persistent whole-school factors, which the DISS project brought so vividly to the surface. In these schools, TA deployment had improved, as did TAs' confidence and self-efficacy, teachers' understanding of the TA role, and a clearer sense of collective purpose evolved (Maxwell et al. 2019). These findings are echoed encouragingly in the evidence from our MITA Journey schools, and in reports and comments we have received from many other schools that have implemented MITA.

Taken together, the evidence describes the benefits to be had across a wide range of worthwhile outcomes that we know appeal to school leaders: making efficient use of TA capital, increasing TAs' confidence, and changing for the better the school's relationship with its TAs, and vice versa. This leads us to our final observation about where MITA sits within the debates about 'what works' in schools, and what such interventions bring to the broader and longer-term process of educational improvement.

To reiterate, we do not disagree that in the debates over 'what works', the learning outcomes of children and young people, especially for those in disadvantaged groups, should take priority. That said, there needs to be space within this debate for work targeting the more complex issues that lie further upstream that are known to affect teaching and learning, and which have a confounding effect on pupils' academic outcomes.

This is where whole-school interventions like MITA come in, as they focus on addressing head-on the kinds of longstanding, underlying structural and cultural factors that form the bedrock into which inefficient use of resources and ineffectual practices become embedded. While such interventions are somewhat more removed from proximal classroom level teaching methods – say, for example, explicit instruction – which can directly influence learning outcomes, they have an intrinsic value *precisely* because they attempt to do what these pedagogical approaches cannot do, nor claim to do: tackle the complicated, residual forces that tend to exist at the whole-school level, which cause the operationalisation of such approaches to be inconsistent in delivery and variable in outcome.

Compared with academic outcomes, these structural and cultural factors are harder to define and to capture reliably, and present researchers with a particular methodological challenge (Anders et al. 2017)[1]. However, few would deny that things like school culture exist nor that they exert an influence on individuals and practices within a setting. Indeed, evidence from the evaluations of the two large-scale regional campaigns in Yorkshire and Lincolnshire found that improvements in schools were influenced by underlying factors related to leadership and implementation capacity. Successful implementation was associated with schools where the leadership team were committed, capable, enthusiastic and knowledgeable, allocated time to the change process, and ensured high levels of staff engagement and participation (Maxwell et al. 2019).

Recognising that improving complex systems like schools takes an array of different approaches also means that we must take a wider view of what we count and value as impact. Impact couched in terms of learning outcomes – vital and revealing though that is – does not tell the full story of implementation or improvement. We need additional evidence that provides the essential detail and nuance relating to *processes* of change to add crucial and complementary balance to pictures portraying the *results* of change, which are painted in the broad, black and white brushstrokes of attainment data.

These, then, have been the twin purposes of this book: (i) to describe a deep and thoughtful process of change that prioritises the essential, though often unseen work, of TAs in primary schools; and (ii) to bring it to life via inspiring, real-world stories and illustrative examples. A process that, successfully and diligently applied, can increase the value of your TAs, ensure they thrive in their role, and maximise their contribution in ways meaningful to your setting.

Note

1 To make a technical point, evaluating the implementation and impact of complex whole-school interventions, such as MITA, presents a greater methodological and practical challenge to researchers than measuring the impact of closed systems, such as the structured interventions we discussed in the previous chapter, where the independent variable(s) are easier to isolate. Despite the rapid ascendency of the RCT method in evaluative educational research over the last decade, there is an emerging view that RCTs might not be the most feasible or reliable way of determining 'what works' in cases where an intervention has many active ingredients; that is, a complex programme of work that combines multiple components, covers a range of outcomes, and targets different levels of (or groups within) an organisation, all of which interact with one another (Anders et al. 2017).

TA deployment policy summary: Our agreement on the deployment of teaching assistants

TAs can expect the senior leadership team to:

- Ensure each TA is deployed in a role that reflects their skills and aptitudes.
- Define, clearly and properly, the tasks and duties each TA can expect to be asked to perform in their role, and specify their contribution to teaching and learning at [name of school].
- Provide timely and appropriate training and preparation to ensure TAs are confident and ready to undertake the tasks they are given.
- Avoid deploying TAs in roles for which they are not specifically trained or that are more appropriately undertaken by a qualified teacher. (Some very exceptional circumstances may apply).
- Recognise and celebrate TAs' contribution to teaching and learning, and treat them as professionals in their own right.
- Provide induction and professional devolvement opportunities, supervision and performance reviews commensurate with maintaining their professional identity.
- Ensure teaching staff are aware of their role and responsibility for ensuring TAs are deployed appropriately and are properly prepared for the tasks they give them.
- Train and support teachers to ensure they have the skills and knowledge to deploy TAs appropriately and consistently.

TAs can expect teachers to:

- Be aware of the school's expectations of how to deploy and prepare TAs, and ensure their contribution to teaching and learning is consistent with our whole school aims.
- Know the respective roles and skills of the TAs they work with most frequently and deploy them appropriately.
- Communicate adequate information and instructions about lessons ahead of time, and clearly specify TAs' role in, and contribution, to each lesson.
- Provide opportunities for TAs to feed back after lessons and provide clear guidance on what information should be fed back.
- Respond in a positive and timely fashion to requests from TAs for information about lessons, pupils, curriculum content, instructional techniques, or any other information essential to ensuring their effective deployment in lessons and contribution to learning.

- Not discharge responsibilities to TAs that, as the lead professional in the classroom, belong to them.
- Recognise and reinforce TAs' professional identity and their status within the school.
- Contribute to induction and training, supervision and performance reviews for TAs.
- Request training and guidance in order to ensure they have the skills and knowledge to meet their professional duties and responsibilities as a teacher, including how to deploy TAs appropriately.

The senior leadership team and teachers expect TAs to:

- Act in a manner that upholds the professional identity of TAs at [name of school].
- Participate in the school's induction programme and performance review process.
- Make the most of training and professional development opportunities to develop their knowledge and skills.
- Prompt teachers for pre-lesson information and to ask for clarification where required.
- Perform and interact with pupils in ways that are consistent with what the school expects from TAs in terms of their contribution to teaching and learning.
- Contribute to lesson planning and feedback at teachers' request.

Teacher–TA agreement template

A teacher–TA agreement can help staff specify their coordinated, but differentiated, roles during lessons. Examples of how TAs might contribute at various stages of a lesson are provided, in such a way that they supplement, not replace, the teacher. The version below was adapted from templates used by the staff at St James' Catholic High School, Barnet.

When?	What? (examples)
During the lesson introduction	• Check learning objectives are written in books • Refocus pupils • Ensure relevant learning materials and equipment are out/available
During whole class work	• Use the scaffolding framework to ensure pupils are offered the 'least amount of help first' • Encourage responses from [names of target pupils] • Emphasise key vocabulary; record key words • Model or role-play activities with teacher • Ensure pupils refer to success criteria • Observe and note learning difficulties and achievements and feed back to the teacher
In group work	• If necessary, check pupils understand what they need to do, what they will learn and what outcome is expected by the end of the session • Provide prompts on group objectives and roles required. Give time checks • Note issues, mistakes, misconceptions and difficulties for follow-up by teacher • Encourage interaction with others
In plenary sessions	• Encourage pupils to reflect on their learning. Prompt recall and use of relevant strategies if necessary • Monitor and record responses of [names of target pupils] (note difficulties and achievements)
At the end of the lesson	• Clarify next steps in pupils' learning • Ensure pupils understand homework and are clear about any follow-up required. Ensure homework is written in planners
After the lesson	• Provide feedback on any misconceptions, difficulties, etc; issues with behaviour for learning

References

Alborz, A., Pearson, D., Farrell, P. and Howes, A. (2009) *The Impact of Adult Support Staff on Pupils and Mainstream Schools*. London: Department for Children, Schools and Families and Institute of Education.

Anders, J., Brown, C., Ehren, M., Greaney, T., Nelson, R., Heal, J., Groot, B., Sanders, M. and Allen, R. (2017) *Evaluation of Complex Whole-School Interventions: Methodological and Practical Considerations. A Report for the Education Endowment Foundation*. London: EEF/UCL Institute of Education/ Behavioural Insights Team/Education Datalab. Available at: https://educatio nendowmentfoundation.org.uk/public/files/Grantee_guide_and_EEF_policies/Evaluation/Set ting_up_an_Evaluation/EEF_CWSI_RESOURCE_FINAL_25.10.17.pdf. (accessed 01. 09. 20).

Anderson, V. and Finney, M. (2008) '"I'm a TA not a PA!": Teaching assistants working with teachers', in G. Richards and F. Armstrong (eds.) *Key Issues for Teaching Assistants: Working in Diverse and Inclusive Classrooms*, 73–83. Oxon: Routledge.

Appelbaum, S.H., Habashy, S., Malo, J.L., and Shafiq, H. (2012) 'Back to the future: Revisiting Kotter's 1996 change model', *Journal of Management Development*, 31: 764–782.

Bach, S., Kessler, I. and Heron, P. (2004) *'Support roles and changing job boundaries in the public services: The case of teaching assistants in British primary schools'*. Paper presented at International Labour Process Conference, Amsterdam, April.

Blatchford, P. and Webster, R. (2018) 'Classroom contexts for learning at primary and secondary school: Class size, groupings, interactions and special educational needs'. *British Educational Research Journal*, 44 (4): 681–703.

Blatchford, P., Russell, A. and Webster, R. (2012) *Reassessing the impact of teaching assistants: How research challenges practice and policy*. Oxon, Routledge.

Blatchford, P., Russell, A., Bassett, P., Brown, P. and Martin, C. (2004) *The Effects and Role of Teaching Assistants in English Primary Schools (Years 4 to 6) 2000–2003: Results from the Class Size and Pupil-Adult Ratios (CSPAR) Project*. Final Report. London: Department for Education and Skills.

Bosanquet, P. and Radford, J. (2019) 'Teaching assistant and pupil interactions: The role of repair and topic management in scaffolding learning', *British Journal of Educational Psychology*, 89: 177–190.

Bosanquet, P., Radford, J. and Webster, R. (2021) *The Teaching Assistant's Guide to Effective Interaction: How to Maximise your Practice*. Second edition. Oxon, Routledge.

Brown, J. and Harris, A. (2010) *Increased Expenditure on Associate Staff in Schools and Changes in Student Attainment*. London: Training and Development Agency for Schools.

Buck, A. (2018) *Leadership Matters 3.0: How Leaders at All Levels Can Create Great Schools*, Suffolk: John Catt Educational.

Cajkler, W., Tennant, G., Tiknaz, Y., Sage, R., Taylor, C., Tucker, S., Tansey, R. and Cooper, P. (2007) *A Systematic Literature Review on the Perceptions of Ways in Which Teaching Assistants Work to Support Pupils' Social and Academic Engagement in Secondary Classrooms (1988–2005)*. London: Research Evidence in Education Library, IoE EPPI Centre.

Caudrey, A. (1985) 'Growing role of parents in class causes alarm', *TES*, 12th April.

Coalition for Evidence-Based Policy (2013) *Randomized Controlled Trials Commissioned by the Institute of Education Sciences Since 2002: How many found positive versus weak or no effects.* Available at: http://coalition4evidence.org/wp-content/uploads/2013/06/IES-Commissioned-RCTs-positive-vs-weak-or-null-findings-7-2013.pdf (accessed 19. 04. 20).

Coldwell, M., Greany, T., Higgins, S., Brown, C., Maxwell, B., Stiell, B., Stoll, L., Willis, B. and Burns, H. (2017) *Evidence-Informed Teaching: An Evaluation of Progress in England. Research Report.* London: DfE. Available at: https://assets.publishing.service.gov.uk/government/uploads/system/uploads/attachment_data/file/625007/Evidence-informed_teaching_-_an_evaluation_of_progress_in_England.pdf (accessed 17. 04. 20).

CooperGibson Research (2019) *Exploring Teaching Assistants' Appetite to Become Teachers.* Research report. London: DfE. Available at: https://www.gov.uk/government/publications/exploring-teaching-assistants-appetite-to-become-teachers (accessed 17. 04. 20).

Curliss, A. (2014) 'Berger: NC pay raise is more important than teacher assistants', *News and Observer*, 7th June. Available at: http://www.ncspin.com/berger-nc-pay-raise-is-more-important-than-teacher-assistants/. (accessed 02. 04. 15).

Department for Education and Department of Health (DfE/DoH) (2015) *Special Educational Needs and Disability Code of Practice: 0 to 25 Years. Statutory Guidance for Organisations which Work with and Support Children and Young People who have Special Educational Needs or Disabilities.* Available at: https://www.gov.uk/government/uploads/system/uploads/attachment_data/file/398815/SEND_Code_of_Practice_January_2015.pdf (accessed 17. 04. 20).

Department for Education and Skills (DfES) (2003) *Raising Standards and Tackling Workload: A National Agreement.* London: DfES.

Department for Education (DfE) (2020) *School Workforce in England: November 2019.* Available at: https://explore-education-statistics.service.gov.uk/find-statistics/school-workforce-in-england (accessed 26.06.20).

Dunne, L., Goddard, G. and Woodhouse, C. (2008) 'Teaching assistants' perceptions of their professional role and their experiences of doing a foundation degree', *Improving Schools*, 11 (3): 239–249.

Education Endowment Foundation (EEF) (2017) *Maximising the Impact of Teaching Assistants: Evaluation protocol.* London: EEF. Available at: https://educationendowmentfoundation.org.uk/public/files/Projects/Evaluation_Protocols/Round_10_-_Maximising_the_Impact_of_Teaching_Assistants_1.pdf. (accessed 01. 09. 20).

Education Endowment Foundation (EEF) (2018) *Annual Report 2018.* Available at: https://educationendowmentfoundation.org.uk/public/files/Annual_Reports/EEF_-_2018_Annual_Report.pdf (accessed 17. 04. 20).

Education Endowment Foundation (EEF) (2020) *Teaching and Learning Toolkit* entry on teaching assistants. Available at: https://educationendowmentfoundation.org.uk/evidence-summaries/teaching-learning-toolkit/teaching-assistants/ (accessed 17. 04. 20).

Farrell, P., Alborz, A., Howes, A. and Pearson, D. (2010) 'The impact of teaching assistants on improving pupils' academic achievement in mainstream schools: A review of the literature', *Educational Review*, 62 (4): 435–448.

Finn, J.D., Gerber, S.B., Farber, S.L. and Achilles, C.M. (2000) 'Teacher aides: An alternative to small classes?', in M.C. Wang and J.D. Finn (eds.) *How Small Classes Help Teachers Do their Best*, pp.131–174. Philadelphia, PA: Temple University Center for Research in Human Development.

Fraser, C. and Meadows, S. (2008) 'Children's views of teaching assistants in primary schools', *Education 3–13*, 36 (4): 351–363.

Giangreco, M.F. (2021) 'Maslow's hammer: Teacher assistant research and inclusive practices at a crossroads', *European Journal of Special Educational Needs. Special Issue: Teaching assistants: Their role in the inclusion, education and achievement of pupils with special educational needs*, 36 (2).

Giangreco, M.F. (2010) 'One-to-one paraprofessionals for students with disabilities in inclusive classrooms: Is conventional wisdom wrong?' *Intellectual and Developmental Disabilities*, 48: 1–13.

Giangreco, M.F. (2003) 'Working with paraprofessionals', *Educational Leadership*, 61 (2): 50–53.

Giangreco, M.F. and Broer, S.M. (2005) 'Questionable utilization of paraprofessionals in inclusive schools: are we addressing symptoms or causes?' *Focus on Autism and Other Developmental Disabilities*, 20: 10–26.

Giangreco, M.F., Doyle, M.B. and Suter, J. C. (2014) 'Teacher assistants in inclusive classrooms', in L. Florian (ed.), *The SAGE Handbook of Special Education, Second Edition*. 429–439, London: SAGE.

Ginnis, S., Pestell, G., Mason, E., and Knibbs, S. (2018) *Newly Qualified Teachers: Annual Survey 2017*. London: DfE. Available at: https://www.gov.uk/government/publications/newly-qualified-teachers-nqts-annual-survey-2017 (accessed 17. 04. 20).

Gorard, S., See, B.H. and Siddiqui, N. (2017) *The Trials of Evidence-Based Education. The promises, opportunities and problems of trials in education*. Oxon: Routledge/David Fulton

Halliday, J. (2016) 'Teaching assistants' strike shuts schools in Durham', *The Guardian*, 7th November. Available at: https://www.theguardian.com/education/2016/nov/07/teaching-assistants-strike-shuts-schools-in-durham (accessed 17. 04. 20).

Hansard (2014), House of Commons debate, 18th March, col 227WH.

Harris, J. (2016) 'Teaching assistants on strike: "If I don't fight the pay cuts, I can't look my daughter in the eye"', *The Guardian*, 10th October. Available at: https://www.theguardian.com/education/2016/oct/10/teaching-assistants-derby-durham-striking-new-contracts-pay-cuts (accessed 17. 04. 20)

Hattie, J. (2015) *What Doesn't Work in Education: The Politics of Distraction*. Available at: https://visible-learning.org/wp-content/uploads/2015/06/John-Hattie-Visible-Learning-creative-commons-book-free-PDF-download-What-doesn-t-work-in-education_the-politics-of-distraction-pearson-2015.pdf (accessed 17. 04. 20).

Hemelt, S.W. and Ladd, H.F., (2016) *Teaching Assistants and Nonteaching Staff: Do They Improve Student Outcomes?* CALDER Working Paper No.169. Available at: https://caldercenter.org/sites/default/files/WP%20169.pdf (accessed 25. 11. 16).

Hodkinson, A. (2019) 'Pre-service teacher training and special educational needs in England, 1978–2018. Looking back and moving forward?' in R. Webster (ed.), *Including Children and Young People With SEND in Learning and Life. How Far Have We Come Since the Warnock Enquiry – and Where Do We Go Next?* 36–41, Oxon: Routledge.

Klassen, R. (2001) 'After the Statement: Reading progress made by secondary students with specific literacy difficulty provision', *Educational Psychology in Practice*, 17 (2): 121–133.

Knoster, T, Villa, R, and Thousand, J. (2000) 'A framework for thinking about systems change', in R. Villa and J. Thousand (eds.), *Restructuring for Caring and Effective Education: Piecing the Puzzle Together*, 93–128, Baltimore: Paul H. Brookes Publishing Co.

Kotter, J.P. (1995) 'Leading change: Why transformation efforts fail', *Harvard Business Review*, 73 (2): 59–67.

Kotter, J.P. (1996) *Leading Change*, Harvard: Harvard Business School Press.

Lamb, B. (2009) *The Lamb Inquiry: Special Educational Needs and Parental Confidence*, London: Department for Children, Schools and Families.

Masdeu Navarro, F. (2015) *Learning Support Staff: A literature review*. OECD Education Working Papers no.125. Paris: OECD Publishing. Available at: https://doi.org/10.1787/5jrnzm39w45l-en (accessed 25. 11. 16).

Maxwell, B., Coldwell, M., Willis, B. and Culliney, M. (2019) *Teaching Assistants Regional Scale-up Campaigns: Lessons Learned*, London: Education Endowment Foundation/Sheffield Hallam University. Available at: https://educationendowmentfoundation.org.uk/public/files/Campaigns/TA_scale_up_lessons_learned.pdf (accessed 17. 04. 20).

Muijs, D. and Reynolds, D. (2001) *Effective Teaching: Evidence and Practice*. London: Paul Chapman.

National College for Teaching and Leadership (2015) *Newly Qualified Teachers: Annual Survey 2015*. London: DfE. Available at: https://www.gov.uk/government/publications/newly-qualified-teachers-nqts-annual-survey-2015. (accessed 17. 08. 20).

Nickow, A., Oreopoulos, P. and Quan, V. (2020) *The Impressive Effects of Tutoring on PreK-12 Learning: A Systematic Review and Meta-Analysis of the Experimental Evidence.* NBER Working Paper No. 27476. Available at: https://www.nber.org/papers/w27476 (accessed 01. 08. 20).

Nicoletti, C. and Rabe, B. (2014) *Spending it Wisely: How Can Schools Use Resources to Help Poorer Pupils?*London: Nuffield Foundation.

Norwich, B. and Lewis, A. (2001) 'Mapping a pedagogy for special educational needs', *British Educational Research Journal*, 27 (3): 313–329.

Ofsted (2014) *Below the Radar: Low-level Disruption in the Country's Classrooms.* Available at: http s://assets.publishing.service.gov.uk/government/uploads/system/uploads/attachment_data/file/ 379249/Below_20the_20radar_20-_20low-level_20disruption_20in_20the_20country_E2_80_ 99s_20classrooms.pdf (accessed 28. 10. 20).

Ofsted (2019) *School Inspection Handbook* (Ref: 190071). Available at: https://assets.publishing.service. gov.uk/government/uploads/system/uploads/attachment_data/file/843108/School_inspection_ha ndbook_-_section_5.pdf (accessed 17. 04. 20).

Pye, J., Stobart, R. and Lindley, L. (2016) *Newly Qualified Teachers: Annual Survey 2016.* Available at: https://www.gov.uk/government/publications/newly-qualified-teachers-nqts-annual-survey-2016 (accessed 17. 04. 20).

Quigley, A., Muijs, D. and Stringer, E. (2018) *Metacognition and Self-regulated Learning. Guidance Report.* London: EEF. Available at: https://educationendowmentfoundation.org.uk/public/files/Publica tions/Metacognition/EEF_Metacognition_and_self-regulated_learning.pdf (accessed 27. 07. 20).

Radford, J., Blatchford, P. and Webster, R. (2011) 'Opening up and closing down: Comparing teacher and TA talk in mathematics lessons', *Learning and Instruction*, 21 (5): 625–635.

Radford, J., Bosanquet, P., Webster, R. and Blatchford. P. (2014) 'Scaffolding learning for independence: Clarifying teacher and TA roles for children with SEN', *Learning and Instruction*, 36: 1–10.

Radford, J., Bosanquet, P., Webster, R., Blatchford. P and Rubie-Davies. C (2013) 'Fostering learner independence through heuristic scaffolding: A valuable role for teaching assistants', *International Journal of Educational Research*, 63 (1): 116–126.

Reynolds, D. and Muijs, D. (2003) 'The effectiveness of the use of learning support assistants in improving the mathematics achievement of low achieving pupils in primary school', *Educational Research*, 45 (3): 219–230.

Rubie-Davies, C., Blatchford, P., Webster, R., Koutsoubou, M. and Bassett, P. (2010) 'Enhancing student learning? A comparison of teacher and teaching assistant interaction with pupils', *School Effectiveness and School Improvement*, 21 (4): 429–449.

Russell, A., Webster, R. and Blatchford, P. (2016) *Maximising the Impact of Teaching Assistants: Guidance for school leaders and teachers.* Oxon, Routledge.

Schools Week (2015) 'In Case You Missed It: Top 10 Most Read Schools Week Stories in 2015', *Schools Week*, 25th December. Available at: https://schoolsweek.co.uk/in-case-you-missed-it-top-10-most-read-schools-week-stories-in-2015/ (accessed 17. 04. 20).

Scott, S. (2015) 'The Teaching Assistants Standards report that Nicky Morgan doesn't want you to see', *Schools Week*, 15th October. Available at: https://schoolsweek.co.uk/the-report-that-nicky-m organ-doesnt-want-you-to-see-teaching-assistant-standards-dfe-report/ (accessed 17. 04. 20).

Sharples, J. (2016) EEF blog: 'Six of the best – how our latest reports can help you support teaching assistants to get results'. Available at: https://educationendowmentfoundation.org.uk/news/six-of-the-best-how-our-latest-reports-can-help-you-support-teaching-assist/ (accessed 17. 04. 20).

Sharples, J. (2019) EEF Blog: 'How can schools manage change and make it stick?' Available at: https://educationendowmentfoundation.org.uk/news/eef-blog-how-can-schools-manage-cha nge-and-make-it-stick/ (accessed 17. 04. 20).

Sharples, J., Albers, B. and Fraser, S. (2019) *Putting Evidence to Work: A School's Guide to Implementation. Guidance Report.* Available at: https://educationendowmentfoundation.org.uk/tools/ guidance-reports/a-schools-guide-to-implementation/ (accessed 17.04.20).

Sharples, J., Webster, R. and Blatchford, P. (2018) *Making Best Use of Teaching Assistants. Guidance Report*. Second edition. Available at: https://educationendowmentfoundation.org.uk/p ublic/files/Publications/Teaching_Assistants/TA_Guidance_Report_MakingBestUseOfTeachi ngAssistants-Printable.pdf (accessed 17. 04. 20).

Sibieta, L. and Sianesi, B. (2019) *Impact Evaluation of the South West Yorkshire Teaching Assistants Scale-up Campaign*, London: Education Endowment Foundation/Institute of Fiscal Studies. Available at: https://educationendowmentfoundation.org.uk/public/files/Campaigns/TA_camp aign_IFS_report.pdf (accessed 17. 04. 20).

Slavin, R. (2016) Blog: 'Trans-Atlantic Concord: Tutoring by Paraprofessionals Works'. Available at: https://robertslavinsblog.wordpress.com/2016/03/03/trans-atlantic-concord-tutoring-by-pa raprofessionals-works/ (accessed 17. 04. 20).

Speck, D. (2020) 'Our TAs stopped the school closing in lockdown', *TES*, 26th June. Available at: https://www.tes.com/news/our-tas-stopped-school-closing-lockdown (accessed 26. 06. 20).

Speck, D. (2019) 'New education secretary shows "unusual empathy" for TAs', *TES*, 29th August. Available at: https://www.tes.com/news/new-education-secretary-shows-unusual-empathy-tas (accessed 17. 04. 20).

Stouten, J., Rousseau, D. and De Cremer, D. (2018) 'Successful organizational change: Integrating the management practice and scholarly literatures', *Academy of Management Annals*, 12 (2): 752–788.

Thomas, G. (1992) *Effective Classroom Teamwork: Support or Intrusion?* Oxon: Routledge.

Walker, M., Nelson, J., Bradshaw, S. with Brown, C. (2019) *Teachers' Engagement With Research: What Do We Know? A Research Briefing*. London: Education Endowment Foundation /National Foundation for Educational Research. Available at: https://educationendowmentfoundation.org. uk/public/files/Evaluation/Teachers_engagement_with_research_Research_Brief_JK.pdf (accessed 01. 09. 20).

Webster, R. (2014) '2014 Code of Practice: How research evidence on the role and impact of teaching assistants can inform professional practice', *Educational Psychology and Practice*, 30 (3): 232–237.

Webster, R. (2015) 'The classroom experiences of pupils with special educational needs in mainstream primary schools – 1976 to 2012. What do data from systematic observation studies reveal about pupils' educational experiences over time?', *British Educational Research Journal*, 41 (6): 992–1009.

Webster, R. (2019) 'Leading without limits: The role of school culture in implementing evidence-based practices', *Impact*, 5: 6–9.

Webster, R. and Blatchford, P. (2017) *The Special Educational Needs in Secondary Education (SENSE) Study. Final Report. A Study of the Teaching and Support Experienced by Pupils With Statements and Education, Health and Care Plans in Mainstream and Special Schools*. Available at: https://discovery. ucl.ac.uk/id/eprint/10096865/ (accessed 02. 10. 20).

Webster, R. and Blatchford, P. (2013) 'The educational experiences of pupils with a Statement for special educational needs in mainstream primary schools. Results from a systematic observation study', *European Journal of Special Needs Education*, 28 (4): 463–479.

Webster, R. and Blatchford, P. (2015) 'Worlds apart? The nature and quality of the educational experiences of pupils with a Statement for special educational needs in mainstream primary schools', *British Educational Research Journal*, 41 (2): 324–342.

Webster, R. and Blatchford, P. (2019) 'Making sense of "teaching", "support" and "differentiation": The educational experiences of pupils with Education, Health and Care Plans and Statements in mainstream secondary schools', *European Journal of Special Needs Education*, 34 (1): 98–113.

Webster, R., Blatchford, P. and Russell, A. (2013) 'Challenging and changing how schools use teaching assistants: Findings from the Effective Deployment of Teaching Assistants project', *School Leadership and Management*, 33 (1): 78–96.

Webster, R., Blatchford, P., Bassett, P., Brown, P., Martin, C. and Russell, A. (2010) 'Double standards and first principles: Framing teaching assistant support for pupils with special educational needs', *European Journal of Special Educational Needs*, 25 (4): 319–336.

Webster, R., Blatchford, P., Bassett, P., Brown, P., Martin, C. and Russell, A. (2011) 'The wider pedagogical role of teaching assistants', *School Leadership and Management*, 31 (1): 3–20.

Webster, R., Russell, A. and Blatchford, P. (2016) *Maximising the Impact of Teaching Assistants: Guidance for school leaders and teachers*. Second edition. Oxon, Routledge.

Webster, R., Sharples, J., Bosanquet, P., Franklin, S. and Parker, M. (2020) 'Inspiring and supporting schools to maximise the impact of teaching assistants', *BERA Research Intelligence*, 143, 12–13.

What Works Clearinghouse (2020) 'Welcome to the What Works Clearinghouse'. Available at: https://ies.ed.gov/ncee/wwc/ (accessed 17. 04. 20).

Wiliam, D. (2010) *'How should we use what we know about learning to read?'* Keynote address at Changing Lives: 7th International Reading Recovery Institute, at the UCL Institute of Education, London, 8th July.

Wood, D., Bruner, J. S. and Ross, G. (1976) 'The role of tutoring in problem solving', *Journal of Child Psychology and Child Psychiatry*, 17, 89–100.

Wood, D. and Wood, H. (1996) 'Vygotsky, tutoring and learning', *Oxford Review of Education*, 22 (1): 5–16.

Woolf, M. and Griffiths, S. (2013) '230,000 classroom assistants face axe', *The Sunday Times*, 2nd June.

Index

Page numbers in *italics* denote a figure, **bold** a table and n an endnote

Printed in Great Britain
by Amazon